P9-EDD-338

365.42
Lam   Lampman
              The wire womb

**GLENDALE COLLEGE
LIBRARY**

DEMCO

THE WIRE WOMB

Life in a Girls' Penal Institution

DISCARD

THE WIRE WOMB

HENRY P. LAMPMAN

nh Nelson-Hall
Publishers

ISBN: 0–911012–23–0

Library of Congress Catalog Card Number: 72–90555

Copyright © 1973 by Henry P. Lampman

All rights reserved. No part of the book may be reproduced
without permission in writing from the publisher, except by
a reviewer who wishes to quote brief passages in connection
with a review written for broadcast or for inclusion in a maga-
zine or newspaper. For information address Nelson-Hall
Company, Publishers, 325 W. Jackson Blvd., Chicago, Ill.
60606.

Manufactured in the United States of America

10/79

The girls in this account are real people with only the names and a few details changed to protect their privacy. The events that take place in this book did happen, just as they are described.

The events involving these girls are reports of actual happenings with only the adult characters altered.

The girls are not only real, but fondly remembered. To Jeannine, to all of the girls in this book, and to all of the girls like them who yearn for a home and find only a wire womb, I dedicate this book.

PREFACE

Today, as I write, the Girls' Rehabilitation Home is little different from what it was on that day I resigned. The superintendent is the former business manager, a man without a day of professional training for the job.

Several women, trained as school counselors or holding bachelor's degrees in psychology, constitute the treatment staff. For a few hours a week, a consulting psychiatrist comes in.

The wire fence and the locks remain. And so does the isolation unit, with its basement cells occupied by lonely girls. One perhaps finds comfort in rocking her head; another flails her body against the door; and almost certainly another is lying on the concrete floor, her face to the half-inch crack at the base of the door, begging, "Please talk to me, please talk to me."

THE WIRE WOMB

I

Girls' Rehabilitation Home—that is a euphemism for a girls' reformatory. The prospect of working there was intriguing, but a few doubts gnawed at me from the beginning.

Being needed was important to me, and it would be interesting to become the first bona fide psychologist the institution had ever employed, the first psychologist in the state in correctional work. But though I liked pioneering, I did not like the thought that I would sacrifice the luxury of talking shop with professional colleagues.

There would be only three other men among the employees. One was the business manager and two were grandfatherly maintenance men. That the environment was overwhelmingly female sharply defined the Victorian tone of the institution, the absurd premise being that in the pure society of women, the virtue of errant girls might be patched up. Nevertheless, my presence, as a male of at least average potency, would constitute a break in that outmoded concept, just as my profession would be an assertion that confinement, punishment, and vocational training were not enough.

These conflicts began in me before I saw the place, when I talked with one of the counselors who was an old friend and coworker from my teaching days. The first visit cut deeper my conviction that here was an opportunity to do a great thing, but equally it bolstered my premonition of hazard.

The chain-link fence was ten feet high, topped by three strands of barbed wire; the steel gate was closed. A telephone was hanging nearby. When I dialed 4–0 as instructed by the sign, the operator asked my name and my business. As I was expected, the gate slid open. After I drove through, it slid back and clanged shut behind me.

The grounds before me grew only scattered desert weeds, with a few Eastern shrubs and trees pitifully surviving around the buff brick buildings, but the buildings themselves were new, substantial, and functional. I recalled William Menninger's appeal to the Kansas legislature to provide as much budget for brains as for bricks, and decided that many years would pass before they balanced here. As I drove toward the first building, a covey of quail sprinted across the gravel road and into the brush. The place seemed less sterile because of them.

The road passed along an unused irrigation ditch and an abandoned chicken house, a relic of the days when farm labor hopefully rehabilitated all misfits. Beyond that stood the grey stucco school buildings. School was out at that time, but as I passed the corner, a dozen girls, dressed in gym suits, raced out from the playground onto the road before me, shrieking the joy of the young at liberation from adult control. I slowed my station wagon and they swung toward me to stare.

"Hey look. A man," one of them said.

A statuesque girl with auburn hair walked slowly in front of my car, feigning oblivion of it and forcing me to stop. The others dashed in man-hungry frankness to the open side windows to look in.

A pixie brunette, about fourteen, led the assault by opening the door. "Hi. What are you doing here?"

"Hello. Well, I'm a kind of doctor."

"Gee. He's a doctor."

One swarthy girl, wearing an extravagant, sweaty hairdo,

groaned and yanked open her blouse. "Oh, Doctor, I have heart trouble."

I grinned. "I'm not that kind of a doctor. I'm a psychologist."

"Man, me for the couch," said a blonde girl, giggling behind her hand.

The tall redhead spoke now with tolerant condescension. "Psychologists don't use couches. A psychoanalyst does that."

"That's right," I said, thinking how bright she seemed. She was different, not so much tall as proud and poised, even wearing her freckles with fierce dignity. I was enjoying the honest spontaneity of these girls, but in my rearview mirror I glimpsed an approaching car, and I felt uncomfortable about how someone else might perceive this situation. Then I saw the girls stiffen fearfully as they turned. A hard, lean woman in a bulky, brown business suit climbed out of her car.

"It's Mrs. Purdy. God," said the pixie.

The girls transformed themselves. One of them looked sullenly at the ground. The pixie dropped her head in mock deference and peeked out from under long bangs. Some put on stoic masks, and a couple, notably the redhead, blazed with defiance.

Mrs. Purdy walked stiffly. "Girls, where should you be?" she asked.

The tense silence lasted just long enough to communicate hostility, until one of the girls said, "At the cottage. We were just going, but this man . . ."

"Well then, go there, right now. Young ladies do not stop gentlemen in automobiles. Go now."

There was another calculated delay before they began to move. I stepped out of my car, hoping to divert the woman. "How do you do," I said. "Please tell me the way to the administration building."

"Drive straight ahead. You will find the turns clearly

marked," Mrs. Purdy said, eyeing me suspiciously. Every item of her clothing, every drab wisp of hair, and her detergent-blistered hands seemed to accuse me of vanity and sin.

I retreated into my professional dignity with a formal, "Thank you," and pulled away. The "young ladies" were reluctantly strolling away by twos and threes, all looking, and some waving at me, irrepressible, mischievous.

When I passed several cottages, I thought they better deserved to be called barracks. I wondered why functional architecture usually turned out to be so bleak. Several of the girls could be seen working around each cottage, taking in clothes and carrying out trash. They froze into attentive observation like startled rabbits when I passed. I wanted to look back at them, admitting that my curiosity matched theirs, but I could feel Mrs. Purdy's eyes on the back of my neck.

The administration building was indeed obvious, on a knoll which surveyed the grounds. I crunched to a stop on the loose gravel, parking next to a car with the state seal on the door panel, and went in to meet the superintendent.

She was a spinster. She carried an ample body to fit her role as "big mama." She was not entirely unattractive but she certainly appeared mature and disused. I spoke cautiously because I had been forewarned that she was not a professionally conditioned person and therefore predictable, but one who through experience alone had concocted her own peculiar frame of reference and her own mode of surviving here; no doubt, her own psychological system. Until I knew how she viewed life, it was hard to know how to relate to her.

"Our board will want to know about your family," she said. "I'm Miss Loomis."

"I have been married for twenty years and we have three children, two boys and a girl. We like each other's company and do many things together. We are glad to come West for the camping, among other things."

"Well, good. This is grand country for camping. I need to think of my board members one by one. One of them will want to know about your views on religion in our program," she said.

"Religion is one of the more important determinants in every person's interpretation of life, don't you think, Miss Loomis?"

"Yes. Yes, of course. But they might be happier still to know your particular religion—ah—religious view."

"I feel that my view is important only to me. It's the child's view that is critical and must be respected," I said.

"Yes, I suppose so. I trust, Doctor, you are prepared to be cross-examined about your attitudes on permissiveness and discipline."

"I don't know if I'll win their approval, but I've been grilled many times before about it. I do believe in the value of limits and controls."

"I'm sure you do, Doctor. Is there any way I can help you prepare to meet our board?"

"It is good of you to ask. I wonder what *you* would like to know about me, Miss Loomis."

"Well, Doctor, truthfully, I don't feel I have any choice. The board does all the hiring. I can work with anyone, as I have for thirty-eight years."

"Miss Loomis, I would not like to come here unless I felt you truly wanted me, that I was your choice."

"Thank you, Doctor. I appreciate that and I will be very happy if the board does approve you. It is obvious that you are intelligent because of your education but I'm glad you are considerate and gentle, too."

She briefed me in detail about the board, and I felt we were colleagues already, working together.

Presently Miss Loomis began to appear distracted by other anxieties, so I relieved her by withdrawing, but not until she made it clear that I was to appear before the governing board on the following Monday evening.

At her suggestion, I toured part of the plant with a counselor. Much of the tour consisted of searching for the right key among a long chain of them, or waiting for someone to unlock a massive door. No expense had been spared for locks, doors, and rip-proof screen windows, nor above all, for the fence; $37,000 worth of fence, she told me.

I met three counselors. Miss Swanson and I had taught together years before in a small town high school. It was good to see her again. The others were earnest and frightened young women with new bachelor's degrees. The nurse was professionally formal and unwilling to commit herself to anything except consultation with the M.D.; several housemothers seemed to be warm old ladies competing with each other at being motherly, and then there were several perennially exhausted teachers. Every department was guarding its own domain, suspicious of inadequacy, wanting help but afraid of censure. I tried to be understanding, and not so professional as to threaten them.

I was not unhappy with the talents of this staff. Their interest was intense and I felt we could learn to work together. Yet, I sensed something was curiously missing, and reflecting upon it, became aware that I had not met one married woman graced with the bloom of mature love. They were spinsters, widows, or very young women. Chastity—that was the criterion for employment here. I couldn't qualify.

Here on this barren hill, behind these locked gates and doors, among these chaste and frightened ladies, were the explosive little girls who had challenged society and been sentenced "until the age of twenty-one or further order of the court." Everywhere their eyes sought me out. I was male, so their eyes blazed hatred, or challenged to conquest, or seduced, or pled for fathering, or most of all, wondered at the strangeness of the differences between us and what it meant to them.

At five fifteen, dinner was served. We were in Pickens Hall (named for a former board member), and we were invited to stay for the meal. We sat at one table with the housemother, an assistant housemother, the cook, and the nurse, exchanging very polite and constrained conversation because twenty girls sat at nearby tables in enforced silence during their meal. When they whispered, the housemother banged a salt shaker on the table and stared threateningly. Talk was stopped, but communication continued. The girls rolled their eyes, shrugged their shoulders, and sniggered and smirked between glances at me, so that I felt thoroughly talked about.

We adults lingered over coffee, while the girls bustled happily into the clean-up period when they could talk. They were busy and it was my turn to study them. I noticed that each girl paraded her problem in some way. A skirt stretched tight across overdeveloped buttocks, or a blouse burst at the button; these were the precocious girls who had been fully developed women before they left childhood. Slutty walks by the vacuous girls advertised the only thing they felt they had to offer. Exaggerated makeup and coiffures proclaimed the conviction that only by rushing into adulthood could a girl escape the pain of childhood. Several tattoos were flaunted as flags of adolescent contempt for adult authority. Mischief sparkled in some faces; there was misery, malice, and madness in others; but from every face there radiated an extraordinary vitality, an energy beyond containment or confinement, a voracious appetite for life.

I suspected that I could not resist this job if the board would hire me. I felt depleted from too many struggles to help many broken older people, with too little time to mend them. Here I saw the prospect of giving intimate personal help to young and promising human beings.

On Monday evening Miss Loomis met me at the door, short-winded from anxiety over her pending appearance before the board, and from too tight a girdle. "It is good to see you again, Doctor. As I told you before, the board of this institution has never given up the privilege of employing key personnel."

"I understand, Miss Loomis. Governing boards are big realities to the superintendent of every public institution."

"Now that I have chosen you, I do hope they accept you. They tend to think of psychologists as being very permissive, and I want to warn you again that they do believe a firm hand is necessary with these girls. They press me to observe every security measure."

"I approve of the firm hand, a firm but gentle hand."

"I know, Doctor, I know," she said, bracing one hand against the other for courage. "Shall we join them?"

She led me into a room where the board was assembled around a large walnut conference table. They paused in their discussion and looked up expectantly at Miss Loomis. She introduced us. Mr. Woolman, the chairman, shook hands with a crunching grip; Bishop Elder was quiet and sincere in his greeting; and the ladies nodded politely. Mrs. Purdy I had unfortunately met before, though she made no reference to it. They resumed their business, leaving me waiting, but giving me an opportunity to watch them.

Mrs. Purdy expressed concern that the bill to the dairy had risen seventeen percent during the month of December. Miss Loomis explained that extra baking needs and whipped cream for the holiday desserts had probably accounted for the difference, but Mrs. Purdy felt that fruit gelatin and similar satisfactory desserts were quite palatable without whipped cream topping. At Mr. Woolman's suggestion, payment of the bill was approved with a caution to the cooks about orders for extra, fancy things.

I knew this board was appointed by the governor of the State, three of the appointments being political rewards for party work or party contributions. One board member was from the opposition party, so the board could be described as bipartisan; but, Bishop Elder's presence there actually made it nonpartisan. Or, so it seemed. A newspaper editorial had described this board as a statesmanlike improvement over previous appointments. As I watched them fussing their way through administrative details, I did not dare to contemplate the past.

Miss Loomis asked approval to have one of the teachers supervise Saturday afternoon recreation. Mrs. Kittredge touched fingertips to her party hairdo, looked archly at me to make sure I noticed, and wondered what kind of recreation was proposed. She had found, in her experience as a recreation worker for U.S.O., that volleyball produced much wider participation than basketball. Having satisfied herself that her coiffure was in place, she smoothed her snug dress over her thighs.

To indicate that she seconded the opinion, Mabel Anderson, who sat next to Mrs. Kittredge, nodded so vigorously that her ample bosom bobbled.

Bishop Elder asked if the physical education instructor was available Saturday afternoons, and finding that she was, wondered if she might not be trusted to plan a suitable program. He moved the approval of Miss Loomis' request, but Mrs. Purdy believed that all Saturday afternoon recreation privileges should depend upon the thorough completion of cleaning tasks. She did not proclaim that cleanliness was next to godliness, but she compressed her lips and spoke with a self-righteous aggression that reminded me unhappily of my fifth grade teacher. Curiously though, I noticed that she had regular features and shapely hands, and might be a pretty woman if she did not so rigorously avoid all vanity.

When Miss Loomis assured Mrs. Purdy that all of Saturday morning was devoted to housecleaning and laundry, Mrs. Purdy was not satisfied. However, Mr. Woolman, who felt the kids ought to have a little fun, said, "All in favor, say aye. What is the pleasures of the board?"

The bishop then wished to suggest that the board consider employing the Protestant chaplain for additional time to provide more counseling services for the girls. Religious counseling, he felt, was in some ways the Protestant equivalent of the confessional. There appeared to be agreement to his suggestion, but no motion was made, and after an awkward silence, Mr. Woolman said, "Let's put this into consideration until the next meeting." He ran his hand over his fuzzy, bald head as though relieved that he had solved the parliamentary problem. I found myself admiring Bishop Elder for the complete respect with which he treated Mr. Woolman, ignoring the malapropisms. Only by letting air into his oversized clerical collar with one finger did he betray any frustration.

Mrs. Kittredge dangled one hand before her, displaying her well-manicured nails, and said, "I know I may be stupid, but—" Mabel Anderson nodded vigorously "—but, I would like to have the business manager come to the next meeting and explain the budget to us in detail. The accounting terms used in his summary meant absolutely nothing to me."

Bishop Elder, giving her a deference adequate for visiting royalty, felt all of them needed help to understand just as Mrs. Kittredge did.

There was no apparent agenda for this meeting, not even a distinction between old muddling and new muddling, but after an hour-and-a-half, Lola Kittredge suggested that they had kept me waiting too long.

Mr. Woolman turned to Miss Loomis. "Madame Superintendent, do you have a recommend for us?"

"Yes, Mr. Chairman." She read precisely and slowly from

a prepared statement. "The Governor's Commission on the Improvement of State Institutions recommended last fall that we consider the addition of persons from certain professions to our staff, among them a psychologist. I have done so, and after reviewing the credentials of a number of persons, I should like to recommend to the board the employment of this psychologist. Copies of his credentials are there in the folder before you. He fails to meet my requirements in only one respect. He is, I am afraid, a man. Perhaps he can persuade us to overlook this handicap."

Mr. Woolman said, "Well, young man, do you think you can work with all these here women?"

I liked the masculine bond he had suggested between us. He wasn't literate, but he was likeable.

"With your help and Bishop Elder's help, I'll risk it," I said.

"These girls are delinquents, you know. Some of the things they have done can make your hair stand on end. There are 147 of them."

"I know, Mr. Woolman. It is my profession to help people in trouble."

"Well," he said with a wide, free swing of his cigar, "you're certainly welcome to try."

Bishop Elder lifted his leonine head from the credentials and removed his glasses. "Doctor, this institution has been moving rapidly in the last few years from a philosophy of punishment to one of rehabilitation, even changing the name a year ago to 'Rehabilitation Home.' Our board has been commissioned by the governor to do just that. We are not always sure how to implement this goal, how to translate the vision into action. No doubt you have much to offer us." He spoke with bishoply assurance up to this point but now he appealed respectfully for my response. "How—what are some of your convictions?"

"I am sure, Bishop Elder, that your goals and mine are entirely compatible. I think it would be rash of me to have any very specific recommendations for this home before I know a great deal more about it. My only firm conviction is that it will repay us to understand these 147 girls as well as we can possibly understand them, and understanding itself sometimes brings about remarkable changes."

The bishop smiled and nodded empathically, and I felt sure I could work with him. He passed to Mrs. Purdy who sat next to him, but who did not look empathic.

"Mr.—young man—are you married?" she asked, making a point of the "Mr." thus stripping me of my education and attacking my personal adequacy in six sharp words.

"Yes, I have been married for twenty years, and we have three children, two boys and a girl, ranging in age from five to seventeen."

"You are a relatively young man, and I know that the behavior of some of these young women may be indelicate at times, to say the least. I think you understand me." She glared.

I smiled, as I did understand her. "Mrs. Purdy, I am very happily married. Furthermore, I am, I firmly believe, too mature to be vunerable to children." My smile died on my face from the lack of response.

"That is indeed reassuring," she said, though I did not think she was convinced. Like most puritans, she seemed obsessed with the impurity of man.

"One of your professors wrote us a letter describing your abilities and saying that you specifically preferred to work with delinquent children in spite of the fact that you have had better opportunities in the field of mental illness. I would like to know why you prefer delinquents."

"That is not an easy question to answer, Mrs. Purdy, but I will try. I find it easy to form a good relationship with angry and rebellious children. I frequently admire their courage.

Truthfully, my preference may be influenced by the fact that I was angry and rebellious myself for a period."

"Oh, really?" Mrs. Purdy asked. "You were a juvenile delinquent, then?"

I was making my usual mistake of being as honest with other people as I must be with myself, but a glance at the others told me they felt Mrs. Purdy was overdoing her attack.

"Not exactly. At least, I was not judged so by the court, but for a year or two, I was in conflict with most of my teachers and was once suspended from school." I dropped the subject and tried another approach. "It seems to me, Mrs. Purdy, that when children are under great stress, they react in different ways. Some crawl under the sheets and stay there. Some wet the bed or develop ulcers. Some live in fantasy. When these things happen, we call a doctor. There are other children, among them many who are strong and bright, who display their problems in some way that violates the law. When this happens, we call a policeman, although these children are crying for help just as surely as the others. I want to respond to them with help." I was speaking to the other members as I finished, and as I turned back to my inquisitor, I saw in her gleaming eyes that I had given her the sword for her next thrust.

"Yes, I can see that you are opposed to punishment. Psychologists are known to favor allowing children much room to experiment, to be permissive, as they say, and to disapprove of such measures as spanking and confinement. Apparently you are typical of psychologists in this respect?"

This was not a question. It was a challenge to argument, and her mind was closed. At that moment I knew I should hesitate long and think thrice before agreeing to work here. Mrs. Purdy was more frank than the others in her hostility, but I doubted if any of them, excepting the bishop, were prepared to comprehend and accept me. I had Mrs. Purdy to thank, for

I could no longer deceive myself. If I chose to do this work, I would do it knowing that I entered the job in almost total insecurity.

"Mrs. Purdy," I said, feeling defensive and trying not to show it, "my own view is that children need control as much as they need love, and need rules as much as they need freedom."

"And do you control your own children?"

Mrs. Kittredge said, "Oh, Mrs. Purdy, that's not fair. I'm sure the doctor has lovely children. Doctor," she said, now that she had the floor, "I am so interested in your work, and I don't even know how to ask questions. But I do hope you will keep us informed so we can all cooperate." Her body moved seductively as she talked, and her heavily-colored eyelids opened too wide when she looked at me. I felt uncomfortable.

"I told the governor," Lola said, "I did not have a thing to offer on this board, but I would love to help these girls. Sometimes I just don't know what to do, but I'm sure you will have so many good ideas."

I answered, "I'm sure the governor showed excellent judgment in appointing you, Mrs. Kittredge."

"There is just one thing, Doctor. You must promise that you won't analyze any of us. I'm just a simple ranch girl, aren't I, gentlemen?" The bishop and Mr. Woolman nodded obligingly but with evident embarrassment, and she continued, "It just wouldn't be fair to have a person with your education taking advantage of the opportunity."

I couldn't think fast enough to know what this woman was trying to do and I wasn't even sure I wanted to know, but I knew I didn't like it. I said, "I suppose—I expect that 147 troubled girls will keep me very busy."

"Surely not too busy to talk to us, Doctor," she said.

Mabel Anderson said, "Well now, you'd just be surprised how well these girls are taken care of. It takes $3,800 apiece to keep them in this style for one year, and there is hardly a thing they don't have. Personally, I just hope it comes to some good. Of course, some of them are as sweet as can be and seem to turn out pretty well in their own way. But the others—well, they probably aren't hopeless. What do you think?" She ended abruptly, her bovine blue eyes revealing that she was bewildered by her own confusion.

Lola Kittredge said, "Well, I think the doctor is charming, and I move we employ him on the terms Miss Loomis outlined."

Mrs. Purdy quietly and insistently told Mr. Woolman, "We should, as is customary, make our decision with the candidate absent."

"In that case, Doctor," said Mr. Woolman, "allow us to excuse yourself while we take a vote on it."

"Regardless of your decision, let me thank all of you for your consideration," I said, and retired to the hall to await the board's decision.

In the fifteen minutes while they deliberated, I lit my pipe, wished it were a cigarette, and stared at a student art display without seeing it. I told myself I would be fortunate if the board rejected me. I had been warned by all of my professional friends against coming to a place like this where my work would not be understood. I tried to convince myself that I would be happy if I were rejected. I also considered turning down the job, but finally admitted that I was committed emotionally beyond any intellectual retreat.

Then the bulletin board came into focus. There were a series of landscapes, done by different girls, in tempera and watercolor and some other medium I didn't recognize, landscapes I had never seen in my life because they were black and brown and grey, olive and navy blue, depressed and withdrawn colors. One was a violent exception, a charcoal volcano erupting lurid orange magma.

"God," I said under my breath, and turned my back on the pathological stuff.

Presently an odd thought occurred to me. After two hours of observation, I did not know who led the group. Certainly not Miss Loomis, nor Mabel Anderson; probably not Mr. Woolman although he was chairman; nor Mrs. Purdy; hopefully, the bishop.

I heard the chairs slide back and the door open. Miss Loomis came to me shaking her head and saying, "They voted to employ you at the salary requested, but to give you an initial contract for one year only."

I had no time to comment before the bishop came, offering his hand and a good will squeeze on the arm. "Doctor," said the bishop, "this, I should think, is an exciting challenge."

"I am excited, Bishop Elder. It particularly pleases me that you are on this board."

The bishop lowered his voice. "I think you will find this a good board. We are all relatively new here and certainly see our roles quite differently, but we, we—are finding some unified approach."

Miss Loomis said, "Doctor, did the bishop tell you he is especially interested in pastoral counseling?"

"No, he didn't, Miss Loomis, but I think it shows."

I felt comfortable in the generous warmth of the bishop and wanted to talk some more, but Mrs. Purdy moved in and spoke at length about a nephew of hers whose life was ruined because his parents failed to spank him. I listened politely and hoped to be saved soon.

Chairman Woolman remained just long enough to crush my hand and say, "My pleasures, Doctor, my pleasures."

Then Lola Kittredge and Mabel Anderson approached, Lola gliding with scrawny sexuality and Mabel cruising voluptuously. "Mrs. Purdy, I have a complaint," said Lola. "Whenever there is an attractive man, you always get there first."

"Well, Lola, you'll just have to move faster," said Mabel. "Won't she, Mrs. Purdy?"

Mabel and Lola laughed, enjoying my discomfort and Mrs. Purdy's disapproval. I recognized now that Mrs. Kittredge was a manipulator. She had outmanipulated Mrs. Purdy, and certainly me, but to what end?

"Good night, Doctor. It is so nice to have you with us," Lola Kittredge said as she squeezed my hand. Mabel Anderson followed her out, her oversize bust quivering.

I listened to Mrs. Purdy talk on about children who hadn't been disciplined, how they should have been disciplined, and how she had been properly disciplined as a child. At this point I hoped she would say what she implied, "And look at me," to which I would have liked to reply, "Yes, look at you." But she failed to expose herself and I repressed my urge to lash back at her.

She was still arguing when Miss Loomis led us out of the building, and I sighed in relief, glad to be over the ordeal.

"Thank God," I thought, as I started home, "it's the kids I'm here to work with."

And all the way home I wondered why, with all the educated, helpful people in the state, these peculiar few had been chosen to govern the lives of children in crisis.

II

When I arrived for work, the board had my office ready. It was adjacent to the front reception area. There was a large window in the door. The window looking out the front of the building was attractively draped, but the glass in the door was not. I knew it was possible that I would sometimes need protection from female slander, but this exposure seemed a little theatrical. By contrast, the counselors' offices adjoining mine had an eight-by-eight-inch window in each door.

Miss Loomis assigned me, with some apology, the task of reading all the orientation manuals for personnel. I wondered momentarily if I were being deliberately detained from serious work. Midmorning I was called to see her, and we sat down to plan my schedule of responsibilities. As we worked, I began to feel she did want my help and we started to have confidence in each other. We agreed that I would test and diagnose new girls as they arrived, consult with the counselors on cases of their choosing, do intensive therapy with several girls, and help train housemothers. Her tense mannerisms dropped quickly as I showed my eagerness to respect her leadership.

Before we had finished, Miss Loomis' secretary called her to the outer office where they talked in secret tones. She then returned, looking grey, gripping one hand tightly with the other and saying nothing for seconds, until her tension broke with a deep sigh.

"Well, Doctor, you may as well see us now at our worst. There is trouble in the isolation unit." She collected a string of keys and hastened out of the room, assuming that I was to follow her at a half-run down the hall. She unlocked a door, went down a stairway, and unlocked another door, through which we stepped into a basement corridor, a corridor with ten closed metal doors on each side, each door with a tiny porthole window.

There were hollow reverberations from the sound of a door being banged upon. A girl yelled, "I want out of here. Damn it, I want out!"

Miss Loomis unlocked the girl's door and we stepped into the doorway. The girl had retreated to the far corner with fists clenched, as though to defend herself against attack. The room was eight by eight feet, ten feet high, with a small, barred window near the top. It was unfurnished except for a mattress on the floor and a blanket, the usual precaution against suicide. In spite of her ratty hair and the bruises on her face, I recognized the redhead who had known that psychoanalysts use couches. Her poise was gone, replaced by reckless hostility.

"Marsha, straighten up!" said Miss Loomis. "I won't have you disturbing the other girls. You are not a stupid girl. You know this behavior will not shorten your isolation." She paused to wheeze, and then resumed with a complete change of manner. "Marsha, this is the new psychologist on our staff. If you settle down, I may let you talk to him later."

Marsha gave me a glimmer of recognition and a suspicious appraisal. Miss Loomis confronted Marsha silently for a moment, then stepped back into the hall, firmly closed and locked the door, the keys jingling so that I glanced at her trembling hands. She noticed and pressed them firmly together.

Was this dungeon necessary? I could not organize my thoughts beyond warning myself to reserve judgment.

A little-girl voice said, "Miss Loomis, come talk to me? Please, Miss Loomis?"

The superintendent opened another door and a frail, thirteen-year-old was at our feet, lying with her face to the space where the base of the door had been. The girl arose, clutching at her wet, chewed pajamas in a female gesture of modesty. I walked away in deference, then waited far down the hall, listening to the murmur of their voices.

"I'm sorry that I'm not sorry, Miss Loomis," I heard her say before the door was closed again upon her.

Miss Loomis felt it necessary to explain to me that the girls in isolation had clawed at other girls, or cursed a housemother, or tried to climb the fence, or hidden a weapon, or behaved indecently (sexually, I supposed).

We opened two more cells. In one of them a plump girl was sprawled on her side, breathing heavily and twitching like a dog in troubled sleep. In the other, a gangly girl slouched against a wall and refused to speak, giving us a look of withering contempt. To me each cell framed an etching of adolescent misery.

As we continued down the hall, Miss Loomis shook her head apologetically. "I wish I knew a better way than this. You can see we do need your help with these hardcore cases."

She hesitated oddly as we reached a door at the end of the hall, studied the key in her hand, and with a sigh decided to use it.

As she turned the key and held the knob in her hand, she hesitated, saying, "Doctor, there is a shocking thing in this room. I want you to understand that I have never used this, and it never will be used while I am in charge of this institution."

With that she opened the door. The room was large with a high ceiling. In the middle stood a cage, a gigantic bird cage, human-sized. The wrought-iron bars were worn chest high to a pewter polish from the hands that had clung there. The cupola was circuslike.

The experience of deja-vu threatened me. Here was something out of the Middle Ages, the terror of the Inquisition. A stale odor permeated the room. I struggled to recall the reality of my own time and place. One of the girls whimpered behind us. Miss Loomis pressed her hands on her mouth and looked at me through tears, unable to speak. I touched my hand to her shoulder to share our guilt for being a part of inhumanity, and we turned back into the hall.

While we walked silently past the cells we had visited, we heard a voice singing softly, but with stagelike projection, "Miss Loomis is a God damned bastard. Miss Loomis is a bitch." Silence. Then the corridor resounded with shock as Marsha's body hit the door. The chant resumed. A housemother in curlers and bathrobe came running down the hall.

"Mrs. Janiske, stay with Marsha until I come back," Miss Loomis said.

She wrung her hands, and escorted me back to the front office, where she introduced me to the case files and suggested that I read some of the commitment orders of the judges, and the state juvenile code, basic law for juvenile offenders.

Miss Loomis hurried away. I tried to bury myself in the records, but found it difficult because I kept remembering the basement, and wondering.

By late afternoon in the record room I became thoroughly depressed. With monotonous regularity the judges had declared these girls to be "incorrigible." That meant "uncorrectable," according to Webster. This was legal nonsense since there had been no attempt to correct them except by edict.

With less monotony, but with incredible naivete, the probation officers in their presentence reports detailed the offenses of the child without interest or inquiry into the causes behind the offense. It was an unusual exhibition of curiosity when one of them reported, "I asked her why she had done this, and she said she didn't know."

The files were full of carefully collected information, with no attempt to select what was relevant. Some counselor had devised a form which reported on seventy-three items, among them the plumbing in the child's household, the number of blocks the family lived away from school, and the religious affiliation of all relatives on both sides for three generations. I looked in vain to find evidence of the girl's feelings toward her parents, genetic determinants, birth history, relationship with siblings, and parental attitudes.

In one file I did find a copy of a letter a child had written to her mother, angrily berating her for an insistent relationship with an alcoholic "boy friend." The child's letter was a gem of communication in a heap of otherwise unrelated information.

Under the juvenile code in this state, it appeared that a judge had remarkable discretionary powers with juveniles, power used in the most diverse ways. Some rural districts with small populations had committed forty girls to the home, while the big city had committed only six, and not because of any difference in the incidence in delinquency. One seventeen-year-old girl found in a motel with a boy had spent three and a half years in the home, while the nineteen-year-old boy found in the same room had been sentenced to thirty days in jail—sentence suspended. The nineteen-year-old was subject to adult justice.

The discretion of the judge was to be used for the welfare of the child, of course, but what appeared remarkable in these records was that no two judges agreed upon what constituted welfare. It occurred to me that many indiscretions were committed in the name of legal discretion. Perhaps, too much was left to the indiscretion of judges. It was quickly evident that not one of these judges had special training in family and juvenile work. They were district judges who held juvenile court when the docket of juvenile cases required them to.

I had no doubt that all adults convicted of any given offense would receive a standard sentence, regardless of which court they appeared in, but with these juveniles there appeared to be no consistency except that the judge had unlimited power. I saw no evidence of any child being represented by an attorney, and I found that the juvenile code required none. There was no indication of any case having been appealed. If appeal were possible, the juvenile code made no reference to it. I wondered if there were a body of common law covering juvenile offenders. Probably not. Juveniles were chattels under old common law covering juvenile offenders, as women had been a century ago, and my experience with child custody cases illustrated the common court attitude that the child was property.

It would be one of my long-term goals to help change the laws and the system, but at that time I wanted to get to work with the children. It was a relief when Miss Loomis hurried in, her brow creased with the now-familiar aura of anxiety.

"Doctor," she said, "that girl, Marsha, the one with the rough language, is screaming now. I don't see how she can keep it up, but she has been getting louder and louder by the hour, and nothing we do or say makes any difference. Would you mind talking to her?"

I was on my feet and nodding. It was good to be needed and great to go to work.

"Marsha behaved beautifully the first four weeks," she said, "so well that we even wondered if she belonged here, but that sometimes happens. Then early this morning she had a temper outburst and the housemother was afraid of her. We sent her to isolation, thinking we would keep her there until she calmed down and learned a lesson from it. I know it is almost five o'clock but we would appreciate your help since

Marsha seems ready to scream all night." She hurried away.

I waited in my office and presently heard Marsha shouting hoarsely as Miss Loomis brought her down the hall.

"A witch. She's a witch. She's a stupid old bitch."

Once in my office, as I closed the door, she turned and said plainly to my face, "Miss Loomis is a . . ."

"I know," I said, "you think Miss Loomis is a bitch." I let her know that she couldn't shock me.

"I think she's a dirty bastard."

"And a dirty bastard. Why?"

Marsha sized me up as an antagonist, despite her standing an inch taller than me. "She locked me up."

"That made you angry."

"It made me want to kill her."

"You are very angry about a lot of things, aren't you?" I sat down and watched her careen around the room.

"You damn right, you damn right, you damn right," she said. "Oh, son of a bitch." She kicked the desk but was too angry to feel the pain.

"Would you like to tell me about it? If I understood, maybe I could help."

"You won't understand. You'll just lock me up like all the other bastards. You're a dumb bastard, too. You think you're smart because you're a psychologist, but if you think you can prove yourself by calming me down, you're a dumb son of a bitch."

"I'd like to help you, Marsha, and I really don't think you *should* calm down until you have good reason to."

"Are you ready to concede that I might have a good reason to be mad?"

"Of course you have a reason. There is a cause for everything people do."

She looked at me long and hard, her hazel eyes glinting. "O.K. You're going to get an earful."

"O.K. I'm ready." I grinned and she grinned back for just an instant.

"Where do I begin?" she asked, suddenly becoming self-conscious.

"If you want to get to the point, tell me about your family."

"My damned daddy is a roughneck in the oil fields. He never comes home 'til late because he stops and drinks beer with his friends. My mom hates him for it and when he gets home she yells all night at him. Oh, Jesus. The way she yells." She bit her fist and then talked faster and faster. "Finally, he belts her and then he goes out and sleeps in the car. Sometimes they fight and fight until I want to scream. Once I did scream and they thought I was crazy. My sister couldn't stand it at home so she ran off and got married. My brother joined the navy to get away from home and I'm worried about my little sister. She's getting too bitchy with the boys. The whole family is going to pot."

Marsha stood with her hands gripping a chair back and kicked at the legs as she talked.

"Why did you get sent here?" I asked.

"I ran away sixteen times."

"Where to?"

"Different places. Everywhere I went they sent me home. Once I went to the preacher and he preached at me and sent me back. Then he talked to my folks and they were decent for about twenty-four hours. Then I ran away to my girl friend and that was nice until my mother came screaming after me. Then the girl's parents wouldn't let me stay at their place anymore."

"Then what?"

"Then I decided I'd run away every son of a bitchin' time they fought. I'd go find a car in a used car lot and sleep there. They called the cops to find me and the cops sent me to juvenile court. I kept right on running away and the judge finally said I was incorrigible. I am, but my parents were incorrigible first. I told them I wouldn't stop running until they stopped fighting, and they wouldn't stop. During the last brawl, I found an empty police car and went to sleep in it." She smirked.

"I suppose you told your probation officer and the judge about why you ran away," I said.

"Sure, I told them. They just thought I was making excuses."

"So you got madder and madder."

"Sure. I wanted something done."

"What?"

"Something to change my parents."

"I'll talk to them, but I can't promise results."

"I know that, but at least I'll find out if they are both crazy."

"Do you think they are crazy?"

She thought a moment. "It's crazy to fight like that all the time, isn't it?"

"Well, possibly sick, but not necessarily crazy. Tell me, Marsha, how did you get locked in isolation?"

"I told my housemother to go to hell."

"Why her?"

She pouted childishly for a moment. "I don't want to talk about it. I don't know why I did that." Abruptly she became tall and intellectual again. "Yes, I do, too. I got a dumb letter from my mother, trying to tell me it was all dad's fault. It just proved they were still at it."

"So you took it out on your housemother."

"I know. Do you know why I started screaming so loud when they put me in isolation? I wanted to talk to you. Can I see you again?" She sighed, dropped her head, and felt of her bruised arms. "Why am I so tired?"

I couldn't help smiling. She looked as though she had just survived a riot.

"I'll see you tomorrow, Marsha. I guess you'll have to go back to that basement tonight, but tomorrow, if you feel you are ready, I'll see if I can get you moved back to the cottage."

I gave her my exit cues and she responded with three steps. Then she stood flatfooted with a posture in which I could see her defying the legal machinery of the state, and said, "I may yell some more tonight."

"That's all right, Marsha. You may need to."

"Thank you. Good night," she said and strode down the hall to Miss Loomis' office, where she volunteered to return to the basement.

I had been fortunate to begin with Marsha because success was almost assured. This was the easiest kind of girl to help, although I couldn't offend Miss Loomis by telling her so. There was character, strength, and intelligence in Marsha. She needed catharsis and understanding, and any beginner in therapy should have been able to help her.

I wondered for a moment how so many people could have failed her, but the evidence suggested the answer. They had refused to believe the simple truth when Marsha told it to them. I had seen amateurs do that before, feeling so fearful that they might be duped that they peered and pried for the hidden truth and overlooked the obvious. It was evident that Marsha's family needed help more than she did, and I asked Miss Loomis what Marsha's probation officer and her community had to offer.

Miss Loomis smiled slyly, something I had never seen her do before. "Mrs. Garvey undoubtedly has something to offer," she said. "She has been able to attract five husbands."

A joke from Miss Loomis warranted some response, so I said, "That should qualify her as a premarital counselor."

Miss Loomis put her hand over her mouth and laughed silently, the soft tissue around her neck turning very red. She tried to repress the laughter without success. Finally, she wiped away tears that had been squeezed out by the repression of laughter.

"Forgive me," she said. "I know what you meant. Clay County, I'm afraid, has no professional workers except the usual doctors, lawyers, and possibly a minister, although most ministers are of the evangelical kind."

The judge who committed Marsha, like most judges, had not visited the home in five years, Miss Loomis told me, but Mrs. Garvey sometimes interviewed her girls when she brought in a new commitment. Parents were encouraged to visit their daughters on Sunday afternoons, but sometimes were permitted to visit at other times. Marsha's parents, a check of the records indicated, had not yet visited. Miss Loomis said she would be happy to sign with me a letter requesting them to come.

Mrs. Garvey was due in on Friday with a new girl. She always brought girls on a Friday so she could spend the weekend "shopping and carousing," Miss Loomis said. She set off on a further description of Mrs. Garvey's character. "Her third husband was the district attorney, so she found it natural to become secretary to the judge. Later she married the judge, and when he divorced her, he made her the probation officer. She was from a prominent ranching family in Clay County. She married again recently so I have trouble recalling her current name."

The good lady paused, struggled with herself for a moment, and then brought herself to confess her full feeling. "Quite candidly, Doctor, Mrs. Garvey is totally unfit to work with delinquent children. She does not set a good example in her own life, and she is certainly unprofessional and untrained. Sad to say, she is not alone in that. The salary of the probation officer in this state is too low to attract anyone with qualifications. However, we must work with her, and we shall, for the benefit of these girls. We try to treat her with all the respect due her position," she said.

I became aware that Mrs. Garvey's position was crucial to Marsha. As probation officer she provided the only communication with the judge, and thus determined when Marsha could be paroled. She could have contact with Marsha's parents and could hinder or help there. It developed that she could even determine what privileges and opportunities would be open to Marsha during her commitment. The full power of the judge fell into the hands of most probation officers because they, and they alone, in most instances, communicated with him and interpreted to him.

Confinement was more difficult for Marsha than for some of the other girls. For some it was a retreat, a womb in which they could find, for a time, a sense of security. Marsha was a strenuous and striving adolescent, eager for experience and for growth. Her anger subsided even more quickly than I anticipated. It seemed important to respond to her appetite for new experience. We needed Mrs. Garvey's approval.

On her third interview, Marsha had moved back to her cottage and had fully recovered the pride and poise I had first seen in her. Her hair was brushed to a high shine, and her freckles were subdued under makeup.

"I was thinking about something," she said. "Do some people like to fight?"

"Your parents, for instance?"

"Yes."

"Well, it's one way of being together when they can't do any better."

"Sometimes it seems like they can hardly wait to get started."

"It's like a game, or a ritual?"

"I guess so, something they just have to do."

"Can you tell me exactly how the fight develops?"

"My Daddy is kind of quiet sometimes and Mama is tired a lot. Sometimes she asks him what's the matter, and sometimes she gives a big sigh, and then he asks her what's the matter. That starts it."

"Then what?"

"Mama complains and says practically everything is the matter and Daddy says it's all her fault. She says maybe it is, but he made her the way she is. It goes on like that 'til she says something that makes Daddy so mad he hits her, or he leaves the house for awhile."

Marsha was silent a moment and then recalled something carefully. "What she says that gets him down is something like, 'I'll never forgive you,' or 'Go ahead and leave. I know what's on your mind.' She doesn't trust him. When he stops for beer on the way home from work she acts like he was with another woman. I don't think he does anything wrong."

"Why do you think your mother acts that way?"

"Maybe once he did have another woman. That could be why she says, 'I'll never forgive you.'"

"Have you heard the expression, 'Hell hath no fury like a woman scorned'?"

"That's my mother. She wants to torture Daddy because he once hurt her, and he could pound the house down because she won't let him come near her. She makes him sleep on the couch most of the time. That's funny. I never thought of that before. They love each other. In a dumb kind of way. How come I didn't think of that before?"

"It might be hard to see the love through all the hating and fighting."

"Uh huh. You know, I used to be in a hurry to go home, but now I don't know. I'm a little bit afraid to go home because I might get confused again."

"Yes, Marsha, I think you do need to be pretty sure and stable to live in that house."

"I used to have a terrible feeling at home when the fights were on. I'd feel like I had to run and get out of there or else I might scream, and split myself in a thousand pieces. The trouble is, being here gives me that same feeling sometimes. That was the way I felt that day you found me in lock."

"You were screaming," I said.

"Not really screaming the way I felt like screaming. I guess it isn't possible to scream and completely express a feeling like that. I don't think I will ever be able to stand being trapped. Some of the girls don't mind lock like I do."

"No, some find a curious security in it."

"I know they do. Strange kids. Nice though. That is something I didn't expect. I felt superior to the other girls when I first got here, but I don't anymore. They have their problems and I have my problems. It's strange, but I think some of the girls I met in this place are the nicest girls I ever met."

"I think so too, Marsha."

"That's not what other people think about them. Everyone I knew used to act like a girl who had been here was a horrible creature. Now, I'm going to be from here, and all of these other kids are too. I wonder if we have a chance out there."

"It frightens you."

"Yes," Marsha said, "but not as much for me as it does for some of them. I have a lot of self-confidence. I can go up to anybody and start talking, and keep talking until they know what sort of person I am. If I couldn't do that, I'd be as afraid as they are."

"That is a wonderful ability."

"But I worry that I'll get out of practice. I don't really think people are so different on the outs, but when I can't talk to them, I can't be sure. Now I have that cramped feeling again."

"The locked-in feeling?" I asked.

She walked to the window and pressed her head against the pane. "I like being here in some ways, and I can learn a lot here, but every night when they lock me in I get angry, and I hate that fence, and that God damned little room. I wish I could get Earned Privilege."

"We need Mrs. Garvey's approval for that."

"Mrs. Garvey. That bitch?"

"Didn't you get along with Mrs. Garvey?"

"I guess I shouldn't have called her a nymphomaniac to her face. She just couldn't understand why I hadn't been sexually delinquent when I had all that opportunity," Marsha said. "I might have been, but I was too mad to think of it."

I wanted another's impression of Mrs. Garvey before facing her and considered consulting one of the young counselors, but none of them seemed likely to be helpful. One looked too frightened to share a helpful opinion if she had one. Another appeared to have been badly disillusioned about something and was too depressed to observe well. The third one was habitually cheerful and unrealistically optimistic. Only Miss Swanson, who headed the counseling staff, inspired my full confidence. When we had worked together in a small town high school ten years before, she had proven to me that she had the honesty, the philosophy, the sensitivity and the empathy needed to be a good therapist. She since had earned her master's degree in counseling as well. She stood six feet tall and was fine boned and graceful in the hands, but she had an ungainly walk.

I remembered that all of the young men, as well as the women, liked her and that she was often dated, but she was an instinctive and inveterate counselor. She wound up being the confidante with whom men talked over the progress of their love affairs. She had some talent for making everyone feel that they had always known her and were resuming a conversation instead of beginning one. I felt that way as I consulted her.

"Tell me about Mrs. Garvey," I said. "I need to know how to appeal to her for help with a girl."

She gave me a quick, sardonic look. "Doctor," she said, "I shall try very hard not to be catty. I am thirty-four years old and I seem doomed to remain everyone's big sister. Mrs. Garvey is thirty-eight and on her fifth husband. So, you see, it is difficult."

I tried to manage an expression that seemed appropriate,

but neither sympathy nor amusement seemed quite right. However, it was good to talk to a fellow worker who recognized her own motives.

"I am able to think of only two motivations to which Mrs. Garvey might respond. One is vanity and the other is sex. Take your pick."

I laughed. "I'll try for a third one first, but a premonition tells me you're right."

"Have you met any of the probation officers?" Miss Swanson asked.

"Not yet."

"They are incredible, without exception, incredible. Bobby Sexton, over in the northeast corner of the state, is a lesbian, a butch type who apparently is discreet enough to have no relationships with juveniles, but she is so obvious in every other way that you can't imagine how a judge or a community could tolerate her as a probation officer for girls.

"Plainsville has a cowboy, Jack Corkoran. No one has ever seen the top of his head because he wears a Stetson hat indoors and out. He can barely read and write and he chews Copenhagen. He does have some horse sense, learned from horses probably. He's a cartoon cowboy. I really get a kick out of him.

"Then do you remember the preacher in *Rain* who fought a war against sin because he was so attracted to it? Mr. Tellamon should be cast in the part. He's a witch hunter and a part-time evangelical preacher. He singlehandedly purges his community of wicked girls and never never lets them back into town."

"Aren't there any trained probation officers in the whole state?" I asked.

"There have been at times, but they don't stay long because they get better jobs. I know you think I'm dramatizing, but I am really understating the situation. However, I don't think you will have any problem with Mrs. Garvey if you want her to do something tangible."

"I want an Earned Privilege pass for one of her girls. Later I'll need more sophisticated help."

"She will agree with you completely, simply because you are a man. I'll be interested in your experience with her."

"I'll bring you my diagnosis," I said, standing up, "and I will stay out of the corners."

"You think that's a joke, but it won't be," she said as she left.

The day Mrs. Garvey was to come I tried to calculate a strategy. However, I abandoned the attempt because I always felt uncomfortable when I tried to manipulate people. I thought about that and decided that because I resented being manipulated, I supposed that other people did too, probably not always a justified assumption. Nevertheless, I decided on a straightforward appeal.

In mid-afternoon, Miss Loomis appeared at my door with a birdlike woman dressed in a black suit.

"Doctor," Miss Loomis said, introducing us, "this is Mrs. Ep—ah, Mrs. Garvey, Marsha Mabry's probation officer. I have known her as Mrs. Epstein, so I'm having trouble readjusting." Miss Loomis disappeared.

Mrs. Garvey's appearance was so ordinary that I thought, "This is the femme fatale?" She had bony, but well-manicured hands, small, bright eyes, a sharp nose, and difficulty covering her teeth with her lips. Then I recalled a recent conversation with my wife. It was after we had seen a movie in which all the characters were typed and tagged as usual.

"Hollywood has women all backwards," my wife said. "When a woman is pretty, with a low-cut gown, jewelry, and makeup, she is probably unapproachable. You watch out for women with plain faces, plain hands, and business suits."

Mrs. Garvey took the initiative. "You are new in the West, Doctor?"

"Not entirely. I have an uncle and cousins who live here. I spent a few summers with them."

"Well, I do hope you like us. I'm from Silverton, you know, Have you ever been there?"

"No, I'm sorry to say I haven't been around the state much."

"You must come to see us sometime. We have horse racing, Indian ceremonies, ghost towns, rodeos, summer theatre, and although the average tourist doesn't see it, I could even show you a gambling den."

"It's the Wild West, isn't it?"

"Um hum. We're wild."

I laughed politely. She was taking the conversation where I didn't want it to go, so I tried a change of subject. "How long have you been working with the court?"

"Six years now, two as secretary and four as probation officer. It's just fascinating. I feel so fortunate. And I feel we're all fortunate to have a real professional like you we can learn from. I hope we can work intimately together, Doctor. I understand you are doing wonders for Marsha. She needs you so much. She's a terribly sick girl. The judge almost sent her to the State Hospital instead. I'm so glad she can have psychological help. What is really wrong with her, Doctor?" She had a curious capacity for saying something reasonably appropriate when one knew her mind wasn't on the subject.

"She's a very angry child. If her story is true, she has reason to be," I began. "Her parents have a violent running battle with each other. Marsha has been in protest, against . . ." I looked up and discovered Mrs. Garvey was not listening. She was studying the contours of my mouth. As I continued talking, she caressed her patent leather purse with her fingertips and traced my eyebrows, ears, neck line, and hands with her eyes. I tried looking directly at her to capture her attention, but she looked excitedly back into my eyes until I flushed uncomfortably.

"Like many angry children, she can change quite rapidly when the situation changes," I was saying. Because she was not listening, I shifted the conversation back to her. "What are Marsha's parents like?"

"Quite nice people, really," she answered. "They have a nice home, and they dress her well."

"Have you seen the father and mother together?"

"Oh yes. They came to juvenile court. Doctor, do you think Marsha will ever be well enough to resume a normal life?"

That was curious. Mrs. Garvey really thought that Marsha was ill. I tried to correct the impression, and said, "Marsha is basically a sound personality. The same strength that she used to fight the law can be used to help her cope with life."

"Really? I couldn't do a thing with her. I can understand a girl that craves excitement. Some girls just can't wait to grow up, and I tell them that there is a time and a place for everything. But Marsha did such dangerous things that were no fun at all. It just didn't seem rational."

She was studying my body as she talked and remembering my usual absentmindedness, I wondered if my zipper was up. I plunged to the point. "Mrs. Garvey, it would help Marsha to have the privilege of going into town for church and for other activities. We need your approval."

"Oh, I'm sure that's a very good idea. I'll be happy to arrange it for you with the judge."

"Fine, and I would like to see her parents here as soon as they can come."

"I'll call them tomorrow, Doctor. I do hope you are right about her mental condition."

She took out a dainty notebook and made an entry. I

began to terminate the interview. "With your help, Marsha should be home and doing well in a few months," I said.

"Oh, Doctor, remember, you promised to visit me. Clay County is really a lot of fun." As she went out the door, she brushed by me as closely as possible.

"I'll be hearing from you about Marsha's pass," I said, retreating toward my desk.

"Oh, yes, I'll call. Thank you, Doctor. It's been lovely," she called, waving good-by with her fingertips.

She made it sound like the conclusion of a date. I resisted an impulse to spit. When, a half-hour later, I saw her drive off in her convertible, I went down the hall to find Miss Loomis. I found her with Miss Swanson and another counselor, obviously gossiping.

"Well, Doctor, how did you and Mrs. Garvey hit it off?" asked Miss Swanson.

I was frustrated to the point of disgust and the impertinence annoyed me. "I did manage to get her attention long enough to say she would request a pass for Marsha."

"She won't remember it. She never remembers anything," Miss Loomis said, more nastily than I thought possible from her.

I flexed my jaw muscles to show my irritation and changed the subject.

It distressed me to find my feelings out of control. It could destroy my ability to handle these situations. Was I overidentifying with Marsha? Certainly I was not identifying with Mrs. Garvey. She was like an overage juvenile delinquent in a position of power. That struck at my most vulnerable point. My intolerance for incompetent people in authority had gotten me into trouble before. I knew I could burn myself out fighting the system without doing any good. It took long-term planning and patience to change a system.

I wondered why I was antagonistic to this type of female.

Usually, when I feel hostile, it is a response in kind. In all probability, I resented the way some women deliberately embarrass a man through some form of sexual manipulation. Lola Kittredge tried this gambit, and made Mabel Anderson laugh unroariously. Both got perverse satisfaction out of my discomfort. So did Mrs. Garvey, I decided. It was comforting to have this insight, but the problem of how I was to handle these manipulators persisted.

IV

The next morning I attended a meeting of the state psychological association at a downtown hotel so it was well after noon when I drove through the gate to the Home.

As I approached the administration building, women began to stream out. Some leaped into parked cars, started the engines, and streaked off to the gates. Others ran headlong across the field to the south, where a young, dumpy-looking girl was scaling the fence.

The ten-foot high, chain-link fence was easy to climb, except for the top, across which was strung three strands of barbed wire. The girl was unable to climb over the wires but was squeezing herself through them. As the women approached her, she panicked, lost her grip, and fell through the barbs, tearing her clothing and skin. She picked herself up, and, clutching at her torn clothing, scrambled into a nearby irrigation ditch. By that time, one of the cars drove up. Several women hurried out; they surrounded and seized the frantic girl.

I went into the building, disturbed over the indignity of the situation. Given all these conditions, the girl, I supposed, must be protected from her own foolishness, but somehow it should have been possible to circumvent this humiliation. I was sitting with my head down and my jaw set, when Miss Swanson came to the door.

"Doctor, did you see the running-away episode just now?"

I nodded, and Miss Swanson said, "She's one of my girls and I need help. Her name is Saralee Austin, and this is the seventh time she has tried to escape. Could you see her soon?"

"I can see her now, if you like," I said.

"If you think this is a good time."

"Yes. It sometimes helps to see kids at their unhappiest moments."

"Good. She'll be in the nurse's office now. I'll introduce you." Miss Swanson efficiently briefed me as we walked down the hall.

The girl was on the examining table when we arrived, biting her lip and rolling her head back and forth.

"Oh Mama, Mama," she said.

"Hold still, Saralee. Let me see you," said the nurse.

"I want my mama so bad." Saralee looked up, saw Miss Swanson and me, and covered her face with her arm.

"The scratches are all superficial," the nurse said as she cleaned them. "Saralee had stiches last time, and a tetanus injection, so all we have to do is clean her up."

"Hello, Saralee, are you all right?" asked Miss Swanson.

Saralee nodded. "I guess so."

"This is the doctor I told you about the other day, Saralee."

"Uh huh." Saralee nodded again and took a quick peek at me, sounding and acting like she was six instead of sixteen. She had a cherubic look; her body was round and mature, but her face and voice were like a baby's.

"Where were you going, Saralee?" I asked.

"Home, to my mother."

"You were taking a short cut, I guess."

She giggled, and then cried.

"It must be terribly important to you," I said.

"It's the only thing in the world I want. My mother and my baby," she said.

"Do you think this is the best way to get there?"

"There isn't any other way. I'll never get home."

"Why do you think that?"

"Because Mr. Tellamon said so. He's my probation officer. He said my mother was irresponsible and unfit and that I should be placed in another home." She winced as the anticeptic was applied to her scratches, then she stopped crying and began to shout, apparently stimulated to anger by the pain. "He said I was incorrigible and that my boy friend was a delinquent and he also tried to make me give up my baby, but my mother wouldn't let him. She is not unfit. Mr. Tellamon is mean—he's mean—he's mean!"

The nurse helped her up, pinned her torn dress in a critical place, and dismissed her, indicating she wanted to check the scratches and bruises again tomorrow.

I invited Saralee to my office. She trailed after me abjectly. If there was a brief, blossoming moment of beauty in Saralee's life, it had already passed. She was plain and yet bountifully feminine, small-boned but ample in all the womanly places. She wanted my help and her eyes appealed for it. There was range and emotional color in her voice. "She was a loved child—at least as an infant," I thought.

"What led to your coming here, Saralee?"

"I didn't go to school and I had a baby. Mr. Tellamon didn't approve of that. He's perfect," she said. "He thinks he can push people around just because they are on welfare."

"You seem to think Mr. Tellamon is completely responsible for your being here."

She bristled. "Well, he said I was incorrigible and he thought I was terrible because I had a baby and he acted like my mother was a whore. If I ever get a chance to kill him, I will. You can't stop me; nobody can stop me. I hate his dirty, mean face and I'll fix him so he'll never—." She stopped talk-ing, strangling with anger.

I spoke quietly, hoping to help her get her adrenalin down. "Saralee, you come from a big family, don't you?"

She struggled to regain her control. "Yes, sir, eleven of us kids."

"Each of you is different?"

"Of course. Children are always different, aren't they?"

"How are you different?"

She thought about it. "I'm closer to my mother."

"Why?"

"Maybe because I wasn't with her for awhile when I was little. I was with my grandma 'til she died."

"How did that make you closer to your mother?" I tried to keep her thinking.

"I don't know—I think it made us lonesome for each other."

"Perhaps your mother felt so unhappy about letting you go away that she wanted to make up for it."

"She could have, maybe. Sometimes she used to say that she'd never let me go again."

"It seems strange, doesn't it, that you and your mother have been so determined not to be separated, and yet you have been."

"Yes, and I'm the only one, the *only* one in my family that isn't at home." The tears flooded her eyes. She seemed so lonely, so painfully homesick.

She was getting out of control again, and I felt she had gone as far as she could in that direction.

"What do you know about your father, Saralee?"

"He hasn't been home in a long time, four or five years now. He travels a lot. He travels all over the world. He is a gypsy and he comes from a family of gypsies. When he and his family get together, it's the wildest thing you ever heard.

Music, and dancing, and drinking. And when my father is
drinking, if anybody says one word against my mother or any
of us kids, he whips out his knife and holds it to their throats.
See, the rest of his family don't approve of my mother because
she isn't a gypsy. Oh, they like her, but she just isn't one of
them. I was my father's favorite and he used to take me everywhere with him. Especially out in the forest, because he felt
a kind of kinship with the animals. He taught me—I know you
won't believe this, but it's an old gypsy secret—he taught me
to talk with animals, and I can still do it."

I decided this dream was too well organized; it contained
too much wishful thinking to be psychotic. It was a beautiful
childhood fantasy.

"One of these days—any day—you just can't ever tell, my
father may show up here." She looked out the window expectantly. "You just can't tell about him. Like one time we got a
card from him in Walla Walla, and he says, 'This is the place
the Indians liked so much they named it twice.' He's liable to
want to take me with him if he comes, and he'd just walk out
that gate with me, and we'd disappear from sight—if that's the
way he wanted it. The gypsies, you know, have their own ways
and they've been hiding people for years."

"You'd like to hear from your father, wouldn't you, Saralee?" I asked.

"Yes, more than anything."

"I wonder if we could locate him, and get a letter from
him?"

"Do you think we could?"

"There are ways of tracing people, and Miss Swanson and
I could certainly try. If we found him, he would probably write
to you."

She was excited, but in identifying all of the relatives and
other persons who might know of him, she never mentioned
gypsies. Neither did I.

Once begun by Marsha and Saralee, the flow of troubled girls through my office increased like a mountain stream in the springtime. Some were referred by Miss Loomis, some by the counselors, some by other staff members who caught me at lunch or in the hall to express their anxiety about one or another of the girls. Most flattering of all, the girls themselves began to seek me out, referred by Marsha and Saralee with unrestrained endorsement.

I marveled here, as I always did, at the infinite individuality of persons and their dilemmas. Yet, individual and different as each child and each situation appeared to be, a repetitive theme began to emerge. It became more apparent when I examined my notes. I had long found it helpful in clarifying my thinking about a child to identify her central problem, and to try to state in one sentence, or one phrase, the problem as she saw it. As my summaries began to accumulate, the common theme developed and became increasingly insistent.

Dorene was a "nymphomaniac," according to her probation officer. I suspected that he encountered nymphomaniacs quite frequently because he leered when he said it. Listening to him talk with the women counselors, I noticed he managed to inject a suggestive meaning into every ordinary remark. Not that he seemed predatory. On the contrary, he seemed the sort who got all of his satisfactions vicariously.

The girl was a spunky-looking fifteen-year-old, friendly and talkative, an only child who lived with her young widowed mother.

"Why are you here, Dorene?" I asked.

"I had an argument with my mother."

"Who won the argument?"

"It's too soon to tell," she said, smiling. "No, actually, my mother and I are very close. We've always been like sisters, talking over everything. We never had secrets from each other.

My mother and me even double-dated all the time."

"You seem to have liked it that way."

"Of course. But something went wrong. She taught me right from wrong, with boys, you know, and I was living up to it. Then when I found out she wasn't, I was surprised."

She looked perplexed, thinking about it. "Do you want me to tell you all this?" she asked.

"If it will help you, Dory. It's up to you."

"Maybe it will. We live in an apartment house and I found out Nancy, that's my mother, was going over to this man's apartment across the hall. She said she was going down to the beauty shop where she works, but she wasn't."

She paused and looked thoughtful again. I waited.

"I didn't know what to do. I talked to her about it and she said that Barry couldn't marry her because his wife had an incurable illness and he had to take care of her. Then I found out that wasn't so. So, whenever Nancy went over there, I'd call my boy friend, Ted, and we'd do the same thing. I found Nancy's birth control pills so I knew what I was doing."

The same puzzled expression crossed her face once more.

"Something about all this bothers you," I said.

"Nancy threw a fit when she caught us. She said it wasn't the same thing as her doing it. Why wasn't it?"

"What did you want her to do?"

"Just be my friend, like she'd always been."

"I see."

"We had a terrible fight and didn't speak for days. Then we didn't talk about it any more. She kept right on going over to Barry's apartment whenever he came to town but she grounded me and said I couldn't have company. I didn't for a while but then one night Rick came over. I wasn't doing it with Ted anymore. When she caught me sleeping with Rick, that was the end, because she didn't like him anyway. Then she got the judge to put me here. You figure it out. I can't."

"You can't understand why your mother was upset?"

"You don't understand. I don't think she wants to be my mother. She wants to be my sister."

"What do you want her to be?"

"I don't care. I just want to be with her. I'm used to it that way, like sisters. Maybe she thinks she's trying to act like a mother."

"Maybe," I said.

"Well, why doesn't she just be herself?"

My summary on Dory read, "I just want to share everything with my mother."

Kate was a large ash-blonde known to all of the girls as "Skunk" because her bleached hair, which had grown out two brown inches at the roots, was parted in the middle, making a wide brown streak. She was referred to me because she resorted to physical combat in every conflict with the other girls.

"Kate, other people feel you have a problem because you get into fights. Do you think you have a problem?"

"Maybe. It gets me into trouble. I guess it got me here. Yeah, it's a problem," she said.

"How long has it been a problem?"

"I always fought with my brothers. I was the only girl and I had to hold my own. They thought I was a pretty good fighter and let me play football with them."

"Fighting was a good thing then, at that time," I said.

"Yeah, mostly. Then when my brothers went off to the army and my stepfather came home drunk and beat my mother, I beat him up. That was a pretty good thing too. I'd do that again."

"I can understand that."

"People get medals for fighting. My oldest brother got one from the army and my next brother got one for the golden gloves."

"That's very true, Kate."

"It sure is. It's sure true."

Apparently she wasn't sure I appreciated the truth of it so I gave her some more illustrations where fighting was heroic.

"Yes, sir. It's true," she said, and we contemplated the truth silently.

"But they didn't give me any medals the last time. They sent me here."

"How did you feel about that?" I asked.

"Oh, it was fair enough as far as the law was concerned. But it didn't work out the way I wanted it to."

"What was it you wanted?"

"I wanted to go with my mother to Iowa. My older brothers are all away from home and I'm the only one left from my mother's first family. When my stepfather and mama and their kids went to Iowa, I guess she thought it would save fights between step-pa and me if I stayed with my grandma. I wasn't going to put up with that."

"What did you do?"

"The first night they was gone I went down to a bar and I tore up the place."

"I guess I understand your anger, Kate, but I don't understand why you tore up the bar."

"Well, look," she said, "when you get in big trouble at school, what happens? They call your mother and she comes to get you. Or when you're a juvenile and swipe something, the police call your mother. Any trouble you get into, what do they do? They call your mother."

"I see that. But in this case, wouldn't they call your grandparents?"

"Well, no, because they know my grandparents. My grandpa spends half his time in the drunk tank and my grandma is so sick with arthritis she can't get down town."

"Did your mother come then?"

"Not that time. In a couple of days they released me. So this time I picked out another bar and I got really drunk and busted bottles and chairs and cussed everybody out. Then Ma came."

"So it worked."

"Sure, it worked great. Ma spent three weeks here with just the baby and me. All the other brats stayed in Iowa."

"Three weeks."

"Three weeks. Then Ma took off again. The next time I kind of got out of hand. I busted a bar mirror and the plate glass window and when the bar maid tried to stop me, I bit her on the tit and it took four policemen to haul me in. Those policemen didn't look too good when I got done."

"Did your mother come back?"

"Yeah, she came. But the judge made her pay damages. That broad had a very expensive tit. Ma agreed with the judge that I was incorrigible."

"So fighting worked and worked, but finally didn't work," I said, thinking I had made a point.

"That's true. Finally it didn't work. But this isn't finally yet. I'm giving my mother and the judge thirty days and then I'm busting out."

On the thirty-first night she did bust out and hitchhiked to Iowa. The state of Iowa took over and we didn't see Kate again.

On the back inside of Kate's folder I had written, "I'll fight my way to my mama."

The pretty pixie brunette who had hailed me the first day I entered the gate was called "Franny." She asked to see me one day, saying it was urgent.

In my office she became coy, studying how best to approach me and not saying what was urgent. The record indicated her parents were divorced two years earlier when she was thirteen and that both had taken her, by turns, into their new homes with new spouses and both had decided she was incorrigible.

"What did you want to see me about, Frances?" I asked, having gotten acquainted.

"Well, I want to call my father about a personal matter."

"That seems reasonable if you haven't made too many calls."

"Just one to my mother last week. Both of them let me call collect once in awhile."

"Your counselor is supposed to arrange that, you know," I said.

"Yes, but I want you to talk to my father too. Would you?"

"If you want me to do that, I need to understand more about the situation. Why would I talk to him?"

"I want him to come to see me. He hasn't come to see me for almost two months, and then he brought her with him."

"Her?" I asked.

"Some broad he picked up. I guess they're married."

"You want him to come alone, then?"

She seized on that. "Yes, I want to see him alone. I haven't seen my father alone for just forever."

By now Franny's combination of wide-eyed innocence and mystery made me sure she was maneuvering without telling me her objective.

"Frances," I said leaning forward, "I won't do anything in the way of making telephone calls or writing letters unless I understand exactly what I am getting into. I do want to help but I have to know what I'm doing. How about leveling with me?"

She looked doubtful, so I continued. "You don't have to tell me of course; it's just my condition for helping."

"If you know what I want, you'll probably interfere."

"I can't promise not to, because I don't know what you want, but I don't interfere if I don't have to. I don't like to interfere."

"You promise?" she asked.

"No, I can't promise. I want to understand you, and you need to understand me, too. I want to be completely honest with you and not promise one thing and do another."

She sighed. "O.K. My mother is coming to see me Sunday because my fifteenth birthday is Monday. I want my father to come too. I want both of them to come alone. We haven't all been together since my twelfth birthday, except in court or the lawyer's office or some dumb place like that. I want them to take me out to dinner, and walk around together, and talk together. You're a psychologist. You ought to understand that."

"Of course," I said.

"Just for one day, I want it like it was."

"Just for one day, Frances?"

"No, that's not true. I want it that way all the time. I want my family together again. They aren't happy either. They love each other. I know they do. They just got messed up. It's probably my fault because they used to quarrel about how to discipline me. So I have a responsibility to get them together again."

That the divorce was caused by arguments about Frances seemed improbable. Like many children, her vanity led her to believe she was the center of her parents' universe and that all catastrophes were caused by or directed at her. But she wasn't ready to face that.

"I understand your wanting them together, Frances. I don't know if it's possible, or wise, but I certainly understand your feelings."

"Will you help me do it?"

I thought about it.

"Please?" she asked.

"You must have tried to get them together before, Frances."

"I did," she said, "but I think I did it the wrong way. I used to go with some boys and stay out late and get taken to the probation office and then they'd have to come together to help me out. Once I said I was going to run off and marry a boy so Mama sent me to live with Daddy. Then I said I was going to marry a serviceman who was home on leave and Daddy sent me back to live with Mama. Like that, I kept trying."

"That had something to do with being sent here?"

"Yes. But when nothing worked, I just didn't care what happened."

"I've noticed that when people don't care what happens, it happens."

"You can say that again. But now I care."

"About having them together," I said, "like when you were ten years old."

I decided that I would not dishonestly arrange a meeting of her parents, but that I would try to do so honestly, or if Frances preferred to arrange it, I would not interfere. She had to resolve this problem somehow, probably by eventually accepting their divorce.

On Franny's folder I had quoted her because there was no simpler way to say, "I want my family together again."

Gloria Velasquez, the probation officer reported, had coldly turned her back on her family, preferring her group of girl friends. With Gloria leading the group, they had found a vacant house and lived there, entertaining boy friends for a week before they were discovered.

Gloria treated me with passive indifference that left me knowing nothing about her, so I was happy when her family came to visit. They gave an immediate impression of being warm and gentle people, bringing with them a station wagon load of their children of all ages, all younger than Gloria. I saw the children playing around the car, every one of them bright-eyed and happy. Why was Gloria so bitter? The family spent an hour with her in the cottage day room and then drove up to see me.

I watched as Mr. and Mrs. Velasquez spoke to me, each free to speak, each contributing facts and opinions, thinking together, never at odds nor resentful of each other.

"Gloria lives with my parents," Mr. Velasquez was saying. "Do you know how it is with the Mexican people? She is our gift to them. But she is still our daughter and still we love her."

"I know about that custom, Mr. Velasquez."

"My husband's parents are good people and Gloria has more than the rest of the children because she is with them," Mrs. Velasquez said. Her English was not as good as her husband's.

"Often we have her come home with us and we treat her just the same as the others, but something has become wrong. She doesn't treat us the same," her father said.

"She is resentful in some way, Mr. Velasquez," I said. "Jealous?" They did not react so I said, "*¿Muy celoso?*"

There was rapid exchange in Spanish before Mr. Velasquez turned to me. "Yes, we think so. It could be."

"Does Gloria have friends who live with their grandparents?"

"Her cousin, yes. But her friends, no," Mr. Velasquez said. "Gloria was happy I am sure until she was eleven years. Now it is different."

We parted presently, all agreeing that we needed to understand Gloria's feelings better.

The next day I saw Gloria.

"Your family was here, Gloria."

She nodded.

"How do you feel about their coming?"

She shrugged.

"They were telling me that you live with your grandparents."

"Yes, I live with them." She stiffened.

"How do you feel about living with them?"

"They are very good to me, more than I deserve."

"It makes you feel guilty to have them be good to you?"

"I don't want them to. I don't want them to love me. I want to be on my own," she said.

"I understand that. You tried to be on your own and you don't want to be with your grandparents."

"It's not that exactly. They're good."

"You just don't want to be there," I said. We were silent for a minute. "Your mother and father wonder if you want to come and live with them."

"No, I do not want to live with them now," she said.

"Once you did want to."

"They didn't want me."

"They didn't want you?"

"They gave me away, didn't they?" Her eyes blazed and her voice raised with anger.

Then it came pouring out, Gloria's long resentment for having been given away. "I don't care if it is an old custom," she said, "It isn't old times. None of my friends were given away. They gave me away."

In five minutes she repeated six times, "They gave me away."

I heard the phrases of the hippie movement so often that I was forced to learn the language. Most often the words were a thin veneer of platitudes over a personality that didn't fit the movement. Claudia was an interesting exception. She was a black girl with an Afro hairdo on the day she came. It was shorn tight now but she still managed to capture the Afro look.

For interview after interview, I listened to her tell me of her life with her group.

"We didn't worry about having a pad or where we'd be next week. Like Marty, our guru, said, 'Consider the lilies of the field, they toil not.' What counts is to expand your mind and do your own thing."

Her thing, so far as I could tell, was to take care of people. "When someone was on a bad trip, I was the best one to help them through it. Or take a boy like Jerry. He was so little and so white, and so scared that he wasn't a man, so I padded down with him 'til he knew he was in the clear. 'Besides,' I told him, 'sex isn't important as long as you aren't hung up about it.' "

Claudia never committed herself permanently to any member of the group. "A promise is a prison after awhile. How can anybody promise somebody they are going to love them forever. Man, that's too far out. Even babies pretty soon have their own thing. They aren't going to appreciate having some guy who just happened to be their father have to stick around all his life. You try to put all that together and you would really blow your cool."

Studying Claudia carefully, I discovered that she avoided anxiety by never aspiring to anything. She maintained a curious philosophic calm by never wanting, and hence never "blowing her cool."

I think she regarded me as her pupil because I showed interest in her outlook and she would often give me bits of advice. "Be honest with yourself, Doc. It doesn't really matter about other people. You do what's right for you and I do what's right for me and maybe we don't dig each other's way of doing it at all, but that doesn't matter. There just aren't any rules about what's right."

She seemed to me to live by a code, a morality as fixed

as that of a monastery, but she denied it. She had been sentenced for possession of marijuana and explained, "Two of the guys had this kilo and brought it over to all of us, and when the cops came, everybody took off. I was in the bathroom and when I came out, there were the cops. So I just said the kilo was mine."

"You are here then partly because you protected the group?" I asked.

"No, nothing heavy like that," she said. "What else could I do?"

It was weeks before the separation from her group dimmed her memory and allegiance. As Claudia said, "The scene is beginning to fade from me like I faded from the scene."

Other memories began to trouble her. "I dreamed last night that I was with my father. He had an old pickup truck and he used to haul trash for people and when I was about five years old, I would go with him. Before we threw the trash away, we'd go through it and find different things we wanted. I dreamed last night he found a doll house for me and then after awhile it was a real house and I was wandering around lost in that doll house."

"The dream might mean that you are lonely for your father," I said.

"I suppose so. He left home when I was six years old and he never came back. For years I guess, I used to expect him to drive up in that old pickup and take me trashing."

"Did your mother expect him too?"

"Who knows? All she ever said was, 'Good riddance,' and she wouldn't talk about him. She wouldn't ever talk about anything. When my grandmother died I had to find it out from my cousin. All the relatives went to the funeral like it was Christmas or something and I said, 'Where's Grandma?' My cousin answered me. All he said was, 'Dead.' I can remember

exactly how he said it. 'Dead.' My mother never did say anything about it, not one thing."

"You sound troubled about your mother."

"My mother is something else. When she had my little
brother, nobody even knew she was pregnant. She doesn't talk
with me about anything. I can't remember where I was or what
I'd been doing, but I can remember the day the thought occurred to me like a big discovery, 'People talk to each other,
a whole lot, almost all the time, not like Mama. They really
talk to each other.' "

For Claudia I wrote, "My group is my family. We dig each
other."

There it was—a motif insistently emerging out of the
separate lives of these girls, a theme obscured by their shrewd
use of sex. Whatever the wording of the commitment order,
they were usually sentenced for sexual delinquency or the
threat of it. Yet, they really seemed to show little interest in
sex. They usually prefered not to dwell upon their sexual
experience, and dismissed sex as distasteful, frustrating, and
depressing. They were capable of anticipation but not capable
of fulfillment. The most cherished relationships with boys
were those never culminated.

The girls had discovered that their parents, and the rest
of society, reacted hysterically to sexual threat. Occasionally,
a girl discovered she could arouse adult panic by spending the
night with a boy in complete innocence. The weapon of sex
was used in a struggle to find and hold something more urgent
and precious to them. Their erotic drives flickered only briefly.
Something else drove them overwhelmingly and unabatingly
—their need for a father and mother.

V

Having worked in the Home for a while, I felt more secure.
I knew I was needed, and I knew that the staff and the girls
were growing to depend upon me. My relationships with the
board I had handled so far by evasion. Mr. Woolman and
Bishop Elder had not appeared. When Mrs. Purdy came
around on trips of inspection, I happened to be busy. I had
twice seen Mrs. Kittredge and her friend, Mabel Anderson,
advancing upon the building, and had deliberately avoided an
encounter. But one afternoon, as I entered Miss Loomis' office, Mrs. Kittredge was coming out and we nearly collided in
the doorway.

Her eyes opened wide, "Oh, Doctor." She was dressed
in a suit with a fur collar that swept down to the waist, dramatizing a low neck line, and she struck a pose as though model-
ing the garment. "When are you going to have some time for
me? I've been waiting patiently."

I ignored the personal charm as I did with the delinquent
girls who tried it. "I am happy to talk with you any time, Mrs.
Kittredge." I stood still this time, waiting for her to give me
some clues. She apparently wanted me to think she was personally fascinated; but I felt she was too deliberate, too con-
trolled, and too contrived.

"I really need a little time with you," she said, and when
I waited, she added, "I am personally trying to decide what

I want to accomplish during my term on the board, don't you know. I wouldn't like to come to the end of the time and say I hadn't really accomplished anything."

"I think I understand. You hope to have some rather definite goals?" I asked.

"Yes, like developing a plan for new buildings, or a recreation program."

I hoped my dismay didn't show, but here it was again, the urge to administer, to plan, to direct, to run the show. I was debating how to respond to her when Miss Loomis came through the door and brushed by us.

"You folks may talk in my office, if you like," she said over her shoulder, as she walked down the hall.

"Do you have the time?" Mrs. Kittredge asked as she moved back past the secretary. Obviously, I had no choice.

When we sat down in the office, I was busy thinking how to be tactful. My silence bothered her.

"You most surely do have some thoughts for me, Doctor. You may feel perfectly sure that whatever you say will be just between the two of us."

"—and the Junior League?" I thought.

"It is wonderful that you are so interested," I said. "There are certainly some very important things you and the other board members could accomplish. They involve some rather sweeping concepts and I am debating how to approach them."

She seemed to like the idea of "sweeping concepts." "I really would like to have you trust me with your opinions."

I explained, rather academically, how a tradition had developed, for very good reasons, that placed the burden of leadership upon an appointed executive and how boards made broad policy decisions, but that the development of programs was an administrative function.

"But the kind of leadership you suggest for the superintendent presumes a kind of superperson to do it all," she said.

"Not necessarily. She has a whole staff of people to help her make and execute plans if the board endorses them."

Mrs. Kittredge looked annoyed and gestured in impatience. "That sounds quite utopian, Doctor. I don't think it would work out here. Well, if it did, I can't see why anyone would want to be on the board. I mean, I don't see what good you would feel you were doing."

On her last phrases the aggression faded from her voice and a tension appeared in her manner. After a moment's pause, she said, "I need your help about a personal matter, Doctor. Do you mind?"

"Of course not." Now I was comfortable and tried to put her at ease. "How can I help?"

"It is my eleven-year-old daughter. There is something seriously wrong with her. I can't get her to school. She gets violently sick every morning and when I force her to go she gets even more ill. Have you run into this kind of thing before?"

"Yes. I see several problems like this every year, but I need to know more about this particular case."

"I had better tell you the whole family situation. I was very spoiled and independent when I was sixteen." She explained how she had eloped and married one of her high school teachers. He was determined to make her pregnant, but he was never content without other romances brewing. They had two children. The oldest was a boy and when he was eight years old he went to San Martin Military Academy—it was a family tradition. Mona was the girl, two years younger. Mona was only seven months old when the marriage broke up and Lola returned home. Lola's mother took over the care of Mona while Lola went away to college. After two years there, Lola took a job with the U.S.O. in Europe. There she met an officer in a reserve air force unit, Major Kittredge, and they were married. It was another year before he completed his tour of duty and they came home. By that time Lola was pregnant again and had a difficult pregnancy, so Mona remained with her grandmother much of the time. Mona began the first grade back in Clifton, the small town where she had lived most of her life. Midyear Lola brought Mona home to their new family.

"Her older brother was with you more of the time?" I asked.

"Well, yes, I think I am a better mother to boys and my mother is better with girls so we divided it that way more often. I suppose that is an important thing in our family. We have a large ranch and when my father died, my brother, Brice— Brice Foley, Lt. Governor now, you know—took over the ranch. I have a third interest in it but he and my mother control it. I always felt that if my father had lived, it would have been different. That's contradictory, isn't it? I think my mother was closest to me but she trusted Brice. I don't really understand it, but at any rate, there has always been some special tie between my mother and Mona, while I felt closer to Curt, my older boy."

"Meanwhile you had a baby—a boy?" I asked.

"Yes, Arnold. He's the apple of his daddy's eye, but I don't think Mona has ever been jealous of him. She is a perfect little mother to him. But on the other hand, she looks forward to spending all summer every year with my mother and leaves the field to Arnold. Mona has a sulky personality. She's always pouting about something. I try to find out what's bothering her but she just says, 'Nothing,' and goes off to her room for hours and dawdles over her homework. That's another thing. The teachers say she is very bright, probably brighter than either of the boys, but she puts nothing into her school work. No, that's not quite true. She won't compete. Her grades are very good but she never excells at anything. It's the same with her ballet lessons. She could be good but there's no life in her. She's a horsewoman too, but never tries to win a show. Sometimes I feel like sticking a pin in her. She will not be best at anything. I was the opposite. I wasn't happy unless I was best. I'm taking a lot of your time, Doctor. I'll get to the point."

I shook my head and gestured for her to continue.

"This September she didn't want to come back home. She said she wanted to go to school there in Clifton. We had just bought a new home and I had a lovely new room for her with complete furnishings and she seemed thrilled with it, as thrilled as Mona ever gets. The problem now is she won't go to school. She gets sick to her stomach every morning, and turns as white as a sheet. The pediatrician says he can't find a thing wrong with her and he thinks its something called 'school phobia.' Have you ever heard of it?"

"Yes, as I said, I see a number of cases every year. How sexually mature is Mona?"

"She hasn't menstruated yet, if that's what you mean. She's just beginning to develop. My husband—he's such a kid sometimes—said something to Mona about little green apples on her chest and Mona nearly died of humiliation. She's a little old maid anyway."

"Has she been ill at all?" I asked.

"Not since September," Lola said. "She had a bad case of the flu and was out of school for two weeks. That and a couple of colds, that's absolutely all. I went over to school and I can't find a thing wrong there. In fact, they gave her Bs in everything the first nine weeks, in spite of her absence."

"When shall I see Mona?" I asked.

"Anytime at your convenience, Doctor. I can't tell you how grateful I am to you." She rose now, model fashion, rapidly recovering her usual defenses, as we established an appointment for Mona.

As we made exit through the outer office she said, "Thank you, Miss Loomis, for the use of your office. I mustn't keep you busy people from your work."

"We do keep the doctor very busy," said Miss Loomis.

When we were alone, the superintendent said to me, "Mrs. Kittredge is such a charming person."

I explained to her that we had been discussing, at Mrs. Kittredge's request, the role of the board, and how I had tried to strengthen Miss Loomis' hand.

"Thank you," she said, nodding approval. "This board, I'm afraid, will never assume its proper role. Well, they are a good board anyway, a dedicated group of people, and we should be thankful."

She found a tissue and wiped dust off the corner of her desk. I found myself liking her more as time went on. I realized that, under pressure, she talked in platitudes but in action she was both pragmatic and dedicated.

"They assume the initiative, don't they?" I asked.

"Yes, and I'm sure I should assume a stronger initiative than I do. Perhaps you will help me. I find myself so often on the defensive. Right now I have a proposal from Mrs. Purdy and Mrs. Kittredge that we establish a minimum sentence of a year for every girl. Will you write your reaction to that proposal for me?"

"I'll need asbestos paper."

"I will too," she said. "But here we are on the defensive again. I think perhaps we should make some really long range proposals."

"That is a good idea," I said. "That will lay groundwork for the future, and preoccupy them, and possibly be a smoke-screen to prevent so much day-by-day interference."

So we proceeded with plans for the development of a statement of objectives for the home, policy statements, and long range proposals.

Then she gave me another assignment. "Bishop Elder and I want you to speak to the April meeting of the board. You may say whatever you wish."

"I'll try to make the most of the opportunity. Any suggestions?" I asked.

"I would like to have them understand what these girls are like. They frequently drop remarks that reveal surprising ignorance. Mr. Woolman once called them 'our little sexpots,' and you know how Mrs. Purdy sees them. Once when Mabel Anderson was away from Mrs. Kittredge's influence, she called the girls 'Poor kids,' with pity as though they were just victims."

"They don't see them as complicated human beings, do they?"

"No, and it will take time, but I think you can do a lot of good."

"I'll give it very careful thought. I have a curious situation now with Mrs. Kittredge. She wants help with her eleven-year-old daughter. The girl is withdrawing. She won't go to school. Do you approve of my taking some office time to work with her?"

"I can't think of any time better spent."

"It might work out that way. There are some dangers. It could make my relationship with Mrs. Kittredge worse."

Miss Loomis thought it over. "We don't really have any alternative, do we?"

"I guess that's the way I felt."

"You know, Doctor, when I was a probation officer and much younger, I wanted a job like this because I thought I would be able to make decisions and have great influence over the outcome of events. Now I find that most decisions are simply accepting what has to be accepted. Not always, but much too often."

"I hope you can teach me to accept when I must. I have a tendency to impale myself on the issues."

"Perhaps we can help each other," she said. "I gain courage from you."

Mona came in with her eyes downcast and every muscle in her frail body braced defensively.

"Mona, how did you feel about coming in to see me?"

"All right, I guess."

"You don't have to talk to me. I would like to help if I can." Coming for help is a terrifying experience for many people. Once helped through it, half the battle is won. I worked to help her accept coming to me.

"People don't believe I'm sick," she said.

"I believe you. I think you feel ill right now. If you need to, just get up and leave for the wash room any time. Do you know where it is?"

"Yes, I found it before I came in here."

"I won't make you go to school, you know."

"Honestly?"

"Yes. School is important but you are more important."

"I don't know what's wrong with me. My mother and everyone keeps asking, but I can't tell her because I don't know."

"I know you don't. How do you feel when you aren't sick?"

"Mostly, I just feel sick."

I had moved too fast. She wasn't sure that I accepted the illness. We spent fifteen minutes establishing the fact that she really was ill, that I understood that she was ill and that I had no intention of convincing her she wasn't ill.

"The school, your parents, and the doctor, everyone keeps pushing at you about going to school. It must not be very happy for you," I said. It was clear now that she couldn't admit resentment, so I understated what I was sure she felt.

"I just want some peace."

"You want to relax from all the pressure?"

"Yes, I can't think. I can't even decide whether everything is wrong or nothing is wrong."

I waited. Presently she looked at me hopelessly, so I asked, "If you could do anything you wanted to do, Mona, what would you do?"

"I'd forget about school this year and I'd go visit my grandmother," she said.

"That would help a lot, I gather."

"I just feel safe with Grandma, and I have friends there, and I know everybody. There's a big old tree in the back yard with a playhouse in it and I would go and sit in it for a long time just like I used to."

Now she was embarked on the untangling of her complicated problem. It was, of course, school phobia, with a classic pattern of symptoms but with her own individual life problem woven into it. She was in early puberty and frightened by the flow of her own hormones and the symbols of her growing up, so she wanted to retreat to childhood.

The virus infections reduced her capacity to face life and herself. She was a little nun in a convent suddenly bursting into womanhood and frightened because she was restless in her retreat. Yet, she was a girl, needing to be one of the girls in her group, and was an outsider when she most needed acceptance. Most of all, she was without the constant, loving help of her grandmother to face all this growing up, grandmother who secretly was a mother to Mona in every way that counted.

Children's literature often presents problems children face, and their fantasies about how to solve them. Mona was a would-be sleeping beauty, wanting to sleep through the pain of adolescence to the day of womanhood.

There is a breed of psychologists who would not permit this illness. They see and try to assuage, as I do, the urgent needs that drive the symptoms, but feel the symptoms must be removed by deconditioning, by forced school attendance with rewards and punishments until the school phobia is gone.

I cannot be part of that. Personality is too precious to me, more perhaps because of my Judeo-Christian philosophy than because I am a psychologist, more because I am a reverent pragmatist than because I am a technician. With many of my medical colleagues I shall continue to feel that the cause is more important than the symptom and the patient more important than the cure.

As a matter of demonstrable fact, Mona would learn as much studying at home for a few months, with a home bound teacher coming twice a week, as she would at school. Her social development also had little to do with sitting in a classroom six hours a day. Possibly, she should have the choice of joining her grandmother, being with the classmates she knew, and in the school where she felt at home.

Complicated as she was, Mona was the least of the problem to me. How would I deal with her mother?

Slowly, in three long interviews, against her defenses and rationalizations, in spite of her frustration with the child, Lola began to see Mona as Mona, to understand her physical problems, to see why she withdrew socially, to empathize with Mona's need for her grandmother and the home territory of Clifton and all that was secure and safe. Lola grew more maternal as she talked and presently in a burst of comprehension she broke into tears and said, "I have failed my little girl, haven't I? What do I do now?"

At last I found compassion in myself for her, and I said, "Perhaps, simply ask Mona what she wants."

When Mona came to see me again, she reported she was going to Clifton. "Mama says I have to move back here sometime. I will. I feel selfish because Mama is hurt about my going. But I feel better for me. I called my best friend back home in Clifton and she asked me to visit school with her next week. Maybe I will."

Mona would recover.

The wound in Lola was evident but she came to talk no more. I called two weeks later and got a brittle report from her that Mona was attending school in Clifton every afternoon.

I planned with Miss Loomis how we might build on Lola's wounded ego.

VI

Midmorning one day, Miss Swanson stepped into my office, her eyes agleam. "Step out and get your mail, right away," she said. "You musn't miss the show."

The mail cubicle was in the main foyer. When I entered I saw two giants, a sheriff and deputy, in full Western regalia. Behind them was their female escort, who came along to protect their good names. She was a woman of equal height and greater heft, also dressed in Western garb but without the gun belt. In tow beside this posse were four frightened girls, not one of whom was over fourteen years or ninety pounds, handcuffed to each other and to the deputy.

Miss Loomis had just come out to receive the girls. She won my final loyalty and affection by saying, "For heaven's sake! Let those girls loose. I won't let them hurt you, gentlemen."

The big men sheepishly began uncuffing their prisoners. As the sheriff unlocked the last of the girls, a wiry, bright-eyed brunette, he asked, "You gonna behave yourself?" He stepped back when her hands were free, as though expecting her to attack.

"That depends," the girl said.

"You better or they'll give you to the bogey man," he said.

"You are the bogey man."

"If you were my kid, I'd horsewhip you."

"You think you're man enough?" she asked.

The posse slammed down the commitment orders on the desk and stomped out, mounted their pickup truck, and wheeled off with their fully enclosed metal rack rattling. The girls must have been confined in that rack.

The girls were registering at the reception desk when the brunette said as though ordering a motel room, "We want a room together."

The counselor who was doing the intake smiled at me and said, "I'm afraid we can't accommodate you."

"Then two rooms, me and Evangeline in one and Pam and Angela in the other."

A single commitment order in quadruplicate covered all four of the girls. They were jointly charged with three runaways and three refusals to return to their parents. On the last occasion they had defied the judge, saying they would never return home. I had to wait until they were cleaned up and otherwise processed into the reception unit before I could hear their story.

New girls were required to deposit all of their personal belongings, jewelry included, with the reception clerk for inspection. Only the items in which no possible harm could be seen were subsequently returned. Then each girl was thoroughly showered and placed in a quarantine room for three days while she was examined by the medical staff from stem to stern, especially the stern. Meanwhile they were oriented to life in the institution. All this was a terrifying procedure to some of them. For many it was their first physical examination and for most, their first vaginal examination. For these four girls, the procedure was less an ordeal than for some because they had adjacent rooms and suffered the indignities together.

Angela was the first of the four I chose to see because she was the largest. She appeared to be in early adolescence, just showing the signs of development. She was nearly fourteen years old. Her first response was to settle primly in her seat and look at the wall. As I tried various approaches to stimulate response she compressed her lips, saying very plainly with sign language that she was resolved not to talk, but at least she was reacting to me.

"You aren't going to talk, Angela," I said.

She shook her head.

"Are you all right?"

She nodded.

"Anything wrong?"

She gave the negative shake and relaxed her mouth.

"Sleeping O.K.? Eating O.K.? Feeling O.K.?"

As she communicated, we smiled at each other. She liked this game.

"One of you girls probably will talk to me. Which one? Evangeline?"

Negative.

"Pam?"

Negative.

"Rebecca?"

Positive.

"Why Rebecca?"

"There's no use talking to the kids," she said. Then realizing she had spoken, she put her hands over her mouth. We laughed.

"I'm sorry," I said. "I didn't mean to make you talk. You don't have to talk if you don't want to."

I made exaggerated gestures to indicate the interview was over and then held the door for her. Her eyes sparkled as she made a queenly exit.

I didn't know why Pam and Evangeline were the "kids," because they were as big as the others, but I took her signal for it; Rebecca was the spokesman. It must have been Rebecca who spoke up to the sheriff.

"Rebecca," I said, "do you . . ."

She interrupted. "I like to be called Becca."

"Becca," I said, "do you want to tell me why all of you are here? I know what the court said, but I want to hear your side of the story."

She was dark and lean and foxlike, remarkably sure of herself. "Nobody cared a damn about us, so we decided to take care of ourselves. The kids, they are only eleven and twelve years old, and they are my cousins. Their mother and my mother are sisters and they mess around together. Well, Evangeline and Pam have these twin brothers about eight years old and their mother spoils the twins rotten and spends all her money on them. We think it isn't fair. She makes the girls do all the work, all the washing and ironing and dishes and floors and everything. When they ran away from home, Angela and I knew we had better take care of them. Somebody had to take care of them."

I must have looked doubtful because she leaned forward and said, "Look they aren't very smart. They don't know how to count their money and they don't keep clean, and when Pam got the curse for the first time last week she didn't even know what was the matter with her, so she started to bawl about it. Do you see what I mean?"

"Of course."

"Then Angela, she had to get away from home. Her mother married this twenty-year-old boy and every time Angela's mother is gone, even in the other room, he tries to feel her up. If it were me, I'd break his fingers, but Angela doesn't know how to be mean. She's so kind that she couldn't hurt anything. That's why the kids call her 'mother.' "

"That's interesting. You are like a family."

"Why doesn't anybody else understand that? I'm more like the father because I get the food and set up the stove and things like that. I sort of boss the rest of them. Did the other kids talk to you about any of this?"

"Not a word."

"I told them not to until I cased the situation. I'll tell them you understand and they should talk to you."

"Thank you. How about you, Becca?"

"What do you mean?"

"Why wouldn't you go home?"

"Oh, I'm used to taking care of myself. My father is in Alaska or Spain or someplace doing construction work for the government, and my mother is either shacked up, or in the State Hospital, or drunk, or something. So it didn't make any difference to me. I might as well take care of the others as well as myself."

"How were all of you managing?"

"Oh fine, until the sheriff found us. See, we were living in an old school bus in a junk yard when they caught us. I guess they saw the smoke coming from the stove. Angela cooked and fixed clothes for the kids and cleaned the bus, and I did the shoplifting. We even kept school for the kids. I was the teacher and they were getting a lot better at arithmetic. I got better at arithmetic too because I had to figure out how to explain it to them. The only big trouble we had was getting enough water. Water is heavy."

When our interview was closing and Becca was at the door, she said, "Evangeline has a very bad tooth. How do I get her to the dentist?"

The more I listened to these girls, the more completely I found they had lived out this fantasy. With no real families, these children had established their own. When I met Pam and Evangeline and realized what babies they were, I saw, as Angela and Becca did, that they needed a mother and father. They did, in fact, look to the other two girls as parents, even to the point of obediently brushing their teeth when they were told.

The sheriff and the probation officers, projecting their iniquitous fantasies, heard a little of this story and suspected a lesbian relationship between Angela and Becca. I saw nothing but the developmental closeness of girls this age. Each girl had boys she admired and they talked with each other about their crushes.

This was the most developed family structure I had seen among the girls, but it was neither the first nor the last. Very often they filled the void in their lives by creating a family and vowing loyalty to each other. They drafted curious documents that resembled marriage contracts and birth or adoption certificates, exchanged blood to become blood sisters and blood children, or tattoed a family crest on themselves.

When they found more caring and a deeper loyalty with a housemother or a counselor or another of us on the staff, the mock family dissolved.

Although Saralee hadn't scaled the fence again, Miss Swanson and I agreed that she belonged at home with her mother and that rehabilitation should be done there, not here. Her hunger for home and parent was a physical ache and she could think of nothing else. By surrounding her with substitute parents we could keep Saralee from impaling herself on the fence, but not for long. We had to have visible progress toward parole. A brief trial visit home would be real encouragement, and that required the usual approval of the probation officer, and through him, the judge.

Miss Swanson was not optimistic. Mr. Tellamon, the probation officer, was in her opinion a witch hunter. "And in *my* opinion Saralee is a witch in *his* opinion," she said. "I don't think I should present the request to him because I just can't stand the man. He's a creep. When he looks at me my skin crawls." She shuddered, half seriously.

"Sounds like a personality conflict," I said.

She laughed and said, "Well, it isn't only that. His judge apparently goes along with him on a policy of long commitments, frequently until the actual age of twenty-one."

"We need some kind of leverage on Mr. Tellamon," I said.

"I can't think of any, except Miss Loomis. She is amazingly good with some of these probation officers. She gets along with them, but she persuades them to go along with us sometimes."

When we asked Miss Loomis for her support, I could see that Miss Swanson was right. Miss Loomis agreed with less evidence of anxiety than usual. So we prepared to approach Mr. Tellamon, three to one, to ask for a trial visit for Saralee.

My own critical attitudes toward these probation officers and board members were bothering me, especially since I found myself disliking Mr. Tellamon before I even met him. Was I hypercritical? Reviewing the people I had known in different situations, the teachers, social workers, psychiatrists, ward attendants, and army officers, every group turned up a few unfit for responsibility, but every group also produced many more who were both sincere and able. Their number seemed to be few here.

Some selective factor must be operating to collect so many social culls around delinquent children. Miss Loomis had suggested that the poor salaries were responsible. That could be part of it, but when I considered other poorly paying service jobs and the effective people filling them, I realized something about the nature of this work with delinquents was keeping the healthy away and attracting the sick personality. It was a problem worthy of research.

I arrived for our meeting with Mr. Tellamon just as everyone was taking a seat. Miss Loomis introduced us. We shook hands across the big table but he said nothing. He was a tall, bony man with severe lines carved deeply into his face.

"Mr. Tellamon," Miss Loomis said, "we have planned to

spend this morning in conference with you, and this afternoon to have you interview the girls from your district."

"I am at your disposal for the day," Mr. Tellamon said.

I was startled by the extraordinary depth and resonance of his voice. He spoke slowly and enunciated clearly as though speaking to a large audience. There was a quality of intensity, of singlemindedness, about him.

Miss Loomis said, "I believe we have nine girls from your district here now, and you brought us a new one this morning. Perhaps it would be well to be informed first about our new charge."

Mr. Tellamon reached into a brief case, pulled out a legal document, and read ponderously from it:

> *In the matter of the alleged delinquency of Rita Lombardelli, age seventeen, District Judge John B. McKlinnock presiding, this girl, a juvenile, having admitted to the offences as detailed by arresting officers, and having been previously arraigned on and confessed to similar charges, is declared to be incorrigible, is removed from the care of her parents, made a ward of the court and the state, and is committed to the State Girls' Rehabilitation Home until she reaches the age of twenty-one or until further order of the court.*

Having read the commitment order as an introduction, Mr. Tellamon cleared his throat and orated without a script. "This girl, Rita, began defying her father at the age of fifteen, and he called upon my office for help at that time. Rita insisted upon choosing friends who did not meet with her father's approval, and upon being at improper places at improper times. In spite of my warnings, her associations grew worse and worse. It was unfortunate that she was biologically precocious, and was possessed with a determination to affiliate with young men from the military base.

"During Christmas vacation, one soldier who was home on leave tried to see her every night. He also has a record in my department. I agreed with Mr. Lombardelli that this was not likely to be a legitimate and wholesome relationship, not likely at all. In the face of our explicit instructions, Rita clandestinely met him in the daytime and escaped from her window at night."

Mr. Tellamon surveyed Miss Loomis, Miss Swanson, and me to be sure he had our attention. "Now," he said, "Mr. Lombardelli and I agreed that it was advisable to apprehend them both under conditions which would enable us to act decisively. He and I trailed the young man's car late at night to a parking place in the canyon. We waited twelve minutes before we approached the car. We miscalculated. Quite candidly I was surprised, because there was blood on the car seat, and the physician, who immediately examined Rita, reported that the hymen had been penetrated only recently, and furthermore . . ."

Miss Loomis interrupted, sensing that Mr. Tellamon felt compelled to savor and share every "pornographic" detail and that we were all offended. "Mr. Tellamon, you have offered us quite sufficient information about the nature of this girl's delinquency. I think further details are unnecessary. Tell me, Mr. Tellamon, what is your thought and the judge's thought about the length of Rita's confinement here? I realize that depends on her progress, but it does help to have some idea when we may approach you."

Mr. Tellamon tapped on his file again, pointing out "The order reads, 'until twenty-one or until further order of the court.' "

"I know," she said. "All of the orders read that way, but court releases sometimes come a week after commitment, and sometimes five years later."

"It is my view, Miss Loomis, and the judge frequently accepts my recommendation, that a delinquent, once committed here, is only to be returned to our community when she is an adult, or when she has completely reformed her character."

Miss Loomis was troubled. "In that case, Mr. Tellamon, you may regard us as premature in presenting this next request, but we must suggest what we conclude is best for our children. Please consider this request carefully. Doctor, please tell Mr. Tellamon our thinking."

I reviewed, very simply, our evidence that Saralee Austin needed more contact with her mother, that she was physically ill from homesickness, that her mother could not come to the institution, that Saralee made repeated runaway attempts and could not be trusted here, but nevertheless, could probably be trusted to spend a very short period with her mother. I hoped that my tone of simple concern with a child's unhappiness would arouse a similar concern in the probation officer. I said, "Mr. Tellamon, it is our strong recommendation that Saralee be granted a two-day trial visit with her mother at this time."

Mr. Tellamon drew another sheaf of papers from his brief case. "Doctor, and ladies, I am not a psychologist, but—"

I cringed at the phrase which usually precedes an amateur's attack on my profession.

"—but let us consider the facts. Saralee absented herself from school a total of 217 days in the last three school years. She was illegitimately pregnant, and had a child by a parolee three years her senior. She was apprehended by police officers on two occasions for being on the streets after curfew. The character and fitness of her mother to raise Saralee, and for that matter, the ten other children, are seriously in question. The first child was delivered less than six months after marriage. It is difficult to say how many of the children are illegitimate, but there are at least three. During school days she has been known to keep Saralee home and leave her in charge of her siblings while she went to town. On other occasions, she has been known to be on the public streets at ten thirty in the evening with Saralee, both of them in scarlet dresses."

Incredulous at first, I began to see that this character assassination could go on indefinitely. Obviously the man was ill, but he held a responsible position. How much, I wondered, should I or could I tolerate of this?

Mr. Tellamon breathed heavily and spoke more rapidly now. "The mother has no church affiliation, but three years ago at a revival meeting she made public confession that she was a sinner. She has not attended church since."

I clenched my fists in my pockets, and looked down, unable to look into the man's obsessed face as he ranted on.

"The neighborhood they live in is not conducive to the rearing of children. Both Saralee and her mother spend time in the homes of women who are known to be promiscuous and probably prostitute themselves, while the children go without baptism. As a matter of fact, the standard of living in this household is a matter warranting further investigation. On their welfare check they not only support the children but entertain male companions. They house two cats and a dog—a bitch usually in season or with a litter."

I could no longer endure my silence. "Mr. Tellamon, we are quite convinced that Mrs. Austin is not the most exemplary person, but Saralee has such an overwhelming need . . ."

The man interrupted with contemptuous wrath. "To return Saralee to that home is to litter the streets of our community with morally degenerate, defective and illegitimate . . ."

"My God!" I exploded. "Why don't we just *stone* Saralee and her mother?"

Miss Swanson laughed tremorously and Mr. Tellamon turned a hostile stare on me.

I took a tight grip on my rage and spoke carefully. "I'll try to be more tactful. All of us here have a responsibility for restoring these girls to society. The whole history of penology makes it clear that they cannot be merely frightened into good citizenship nor humiliated into it nor punished into it. If we want to help, we must think how to be helpful. The professional person does what is helpful to the child." I paused and saw the ruthless righteousness in his face. Oh hell, I thought, I may as well speak plainly, and I said, "The amateur allows himself to be sentimental, or sadistic, with the excuse that it is good for the child."

Shock froze the group into silence. Then Miss Loomis nervously suggested a coffee break. During the informal chatter, she suggested to me that the remainder of the conference might go better without me. I agreed with her.

Back in my office, I trembled in fury for an hour over the enormity of the situation. I rode home that night in turmoil. I felt the same regret that followed a just fight when I was a boy, the same vague guilt. It was good to go home and be healed. It was good to be embraced joyfully and see the loving faces of Bonnie and the children, faces unscarred with hostility and the need to hate and to hurt.

I felt a moment of reluctance to share my troubles and to confess that I had won no victories that day. But Bonnie already knew. One look at my face had told her and she waited. I stalled, lighting kindling in the fireplace while I reminded myself that Bonnie was a courageous woman; she only appeared exquisite and fragile. She was a woman with strengths in some ways beyond my own.

After telling her the painful story, I paused. "I may not last on this job," I finally said.

"Do you want to look for something better?" she asked. "It's all right with us, you know."

"No, I don't think I can quit. I've never felt so needed. It's precisely because of the idiotic incompetence of these adults that I'm needed by the children."

"The adults need you about as much as the girls do," she said.

"Yes, that's true, but there's one very important difference. The adults haven't asked for my help. I'm being thrust upon them."

"I see that," she said. "You can't help someone who doesn't want help."

"The psychiatrist who supervised me in the hospital used to say you can't help someone paint a fence, unless he is painting a fence."

"Well, darling, you may be making a lot more progress than you think you are."

"That's true," I said. "I guess I must play it by ear."

I added a log and we watched the fire in silence. Each of the children came in on some thin excuse, really to make sure everything was secure. Bonnie and I smiled over it and I felt very close to her. We touched hands and did not need to say we would endure.

"Well," I said at length, "a lot of people know where I stand. I don't feel very good about this fight today, but . . ."

"But you'd feel worse if you hadn't fought, Sir Launcelot," she finished for me, smiling as she stood up.

"That's right, Smartie." I playfully slapped her shapely derriere. "Are there any good movies in town? I feel the need of escaping from myself."

"On an empty stomach?" asked Bonnie.

"No, I feel magnanimous. Dinner, too."

"I accept. We'll have the meat loaf tomorrow night. There's an experimental play at the Art Colony out in the canyon."

"Good," I said. "I heard of a gourmet restaurant out that way, too. We'll experiment with the food. I'll read to Tony while you dress."

It was a new drive for us that evening. We missed a turn near the edge of town and found ourselves in a cul-de-sac with small shops. At the end of the street and against a hillside was an impressive building in the style of a Swiss chalet. "The Schweitzer Inn—a Residential Hotel," read the sign; and

"Rathskeller" another read over a half-basement room.

"That looks interesting. How about a drink?" I asked.
She was intrigued, too.

I had been preoccupied as I drove, re-enacting and recon-
structing the day's conflict, much as I wished to forget it. But
when I helped Bonnie out of the car I forgot my work. My
demure wife had blossomed into a blazing beauty, as she did
sometimes, shocking me with a dramatic splash of color into
full awareness.

As we walked down the quiet street, I held her hand at
arm's length to see her better. Desire surged in me.

The Rathskeller deserved its name. A bartender spoiled
the solitude, but we sat in a dark corner, and soft background
music hushed our voices. I kissed her fingertips and smiled
into her eyes until she blushed.

We had ordered a second martini when a flashy brunette
of uncertain middle years came in and sat at the bar. She spoke
with a trace of accent. Somehow she contrived to appear mysterious, but she failed to cover her fear of aging and her bitter-
ness. Evidently she was waiting for someone, and my wife
chose to control my ardor by showing interest in the situation.

"She is someone's mistress, probably someone quite important," said Bonnie.

"She's probably the room clerk's wife," I said.

"No, she's not wearing a ring and she has a very professional air."

"You read too many spy stories."

"Shh, here he is." Bonnie said.

"Good evening, Gov'nor," said the bartender.

A man with a shock of red-graying hair, wearing a gray
Western suit, boots and Stetson hat, moved in nervously. He
glanced around the room and slid on to a stool next to the
woman. The bartender poured a double Scotch without being
told. The man spoke in secret tones to the woman.

My wife looked significantly at me. I frowned. "Who is that?"

Bonnie made a face and whispered behind her hand, "It's the Lieutenant Governor, Brice Foley. You know, the biggest rancher in the state."

I took one more look and then gulped my drink. "Do you think we should go?" My wife nodded.

We studiously avoided looking as we left, but felt conspicuous. I saw Foley's eyes raking Bonnie and slipped my arm around her protectively—no, possessively.

"What do you plan to order for dinner tonight, dear?" she asked me.

"Um, I don't know. Do you have a suggestion?" I asked as we walked out the door.

"How about crow?" she said. And then, forgetting all about the Lieutenant Governor's private life, we proceeded to celebrate our own.

The next day I went back to my job rejuvenated by my evening with Bonnie. Work with troubled children was much more than merely intellectual. A day's work often produced a sense of depletion, as though I had been giving blood transfusions all day. How some of my colleagues who were unhappy at home managed to recharge themselves for such emotional exertion, I had no idea.

The reception unit held three new girls and I was prepared to see them. The white haired housemother, Mrs. Winifred, spoke to me in hushed, confidential tones, even though we appeared to be quite alone.

"Doctor, I should explain that these girls arrived yesterday and have no issue of clothing yet. They have nothing but the nightgowns we have given them. That's partly to prevent a runaway, you know. Which girl do you want to see first?"

I had decided to see Isabel Balboa first and said so.

"Isabel has her hair all done up in rags and medicine. Don't ask her about it. Nits, you know." Mrs. Winifred flared her nostrils. While she went after Isabel, I reviewed the scanty information the probation officer had sent us.

Isabel Balboa was sixteen years of age, had disappeared from home and school, and had been found living in a dilapidated trailer with two young construction workers. Her father was a tubercular veteran who drank heavily and relapsed every time he left the hospital. Her mother periodically resided at the State Hospital, diagnosed as schizophrenic. The home was Spanish-speaking according to the record, although I wondered when it was a home and when they spoke. Several siblings had been reared by grandparents, aunts, and uncles, or moved back and forth from parents to "los primos."

Isabel appeared, as expected, in a long flannel nightgown, her hair wrapped in a towel. She would not look at me, but sat on the edge of her chair and stared at the floor. Her eyes were big, dark, and hollow, like a Keene portrait of a starving child; her skin was sallow and translucent, and an artery pulsed beneath one eye so obviously I could count her pulse.

"Isabel, I would like to get acquainted with you, so all of us will know how to help you."

No response.

"How do you feel about being here?"

Still no response.

"*¿Como está, Isabel?*"

She looked at me with a tiny spark of warmth. "*Así, así,*" she said.

"*¿Es el famoso conquistador, Balboa, uno de sus predecessores?*" I asked.

"*¿Repita, por favor?*"

I repeated the question in English and again in Spanish. Her eyes grew blank and she retreated from our contact. She did not know of a famous man named Balboa. How could *any* teacher fail to build her ego by telling her? I couldn't resist, and sketched the romantic story.

While I talked I drew a crude map to show the Isthmus of Panama. "Below Mexico, see?"

"¡Sí!" she said. "¡Senor Balboa uno de mis abuelos!"

She was painfully thin but her abdomen protruded. I debated whether it might be malnutrition or pregnancy. On pure intuition, I decided to ask.

"Isobel," I pronounced her name in Spanish, leaned forward and gave her all the warmth I could. "Are you—¿con niño? Embarazada?"

"¡No sé!" she shrugged. "¿Quién sabe? Sea como Dios quiera."

"Do you want to have a baby?"

"¡Sí!"

"Why?"

"For something of my own," she said.

I found myself hoping she would have a baby, for something of her own, and another beginning for these great people who in four hundred and fifty years had deadended here, impoverished in body, culture, and spirit.

"Isabel, did you bring anything with you? Anything important—important for you?"

"Sí, my rosary, by my grandmother."

"Would you like it now?"

"Oh. Sí." she said.

"I will get it for you. But you must do something for me. Do you like the food here?"

"No."

"You must promise to eat it anyway. As much as you can. You will?"

"Yes."

The reception clerk balked at returning Isabel's rosary two days before the scheduled time. If I was unduly incisive with the clerk it was because I had heard too much foolish talk from psychedelic circles about "finding yourself" in an hallucination. I knew the meaningful knowledge of self depended on interaction with familiar, tangible things, and people, and ideas about them. I got Isabel's rosary.

Billy Joy Kepler was next.

"She's pregnant, over five months along," said Mrs. Winifred, and walked to the end of the hall to get her.

I did not like Mrs. Winifred as I did the other housemothers. There was a taint of hostility in everything she did and her attitude made me suspect she was capable of conspiring.

Billy Joy was tall and raw-boned with a skin already blistered old in the sun. "This is terrible, being talked to in a night dress," she said.

"Where are your people from originally, Billy Joy?"

"I was born on the ranch and so was my pa but his pa came from Alabama and cut out this ranch."

"Do you like the ranch?"

"Well, sir, I like having my own mare."

"You understand that I am a psychologist, and that my job is to try to understand you?"

"Yes, sir. You bit off quite a chunk this time."

"You seem pretty smart, Billy Joy. Why don't you just explain yourself to me and save me the work?" I leaned back in my chair.

"O.K. I mean, yes, sir. I simply don't get along with my father. He says I'm going to burn in hell and if he's right I may as well have a fling first. I'm pregnant by a school teacher, or maybe a preacher," she paused to observe the effect.

"What church do you belong to?"

"It doesn't have a name. That's one of its principles. They just meet out of doors or in people's houses on Sunday and read the Bible and convert each other. My pa is really gone on this religion."

"What do they believe in?"

"I don't rightly know what they believe in, but I know what they are against. They're against sex, and liquor, and tobacco, and coffee, and soft drinks, and movies, and radio, and television, and comic books, and chewing gum, and pretty clothes, and practically anything else you can think of."

"So you are in rebellion against this religion and against your father?"

She sprawled out on the chair comfortably. "You got it right."

"When did your rebellion begin?"

"Well, let's see. I was in a state of grace 'til right after I was baptized. This preacher came to our house the summer I was fourteen. We'd all been baptized in the Methodist Church before—just sprinkled, you know, but in this religion we believe in total inversion."

I choked back my laughter.

Billy Joy continued, "Well, this preacher kept praying and dunking me and putting his hands on me in different places, and dunking me some more, because he said the devil had a special hold on me. That night he caught me currying my mare and made me on the hay." She paused and thought about it for a couple of moments. "I guess I've been in rebellion since then.

"I don't mean I've been in rebellion against being made. I don't know what that had to do with it. I guess it just sprung me loose. After that I wasn't going to let my pa be the dictator. I wasn't scared of him anymore. Well, not too scared as long as I kept working and didn't try to have friends. Have you ever been around a ranch?"

"No, I haven't, Billy Joy."

"Well, a ranch is a place you took away from the Indians, and maybe the Mexicans, or the Yankees. And everybody that comes along is an enemy that's going to take your ranch away from you. That's the way Pa thinks, so everybody is his enemy. All it is, is slavery to me, and I'd give it to the feed and implement company for the lien if they wanted it. If they was smart they wouldn't want it, but Pa figures everybody wants it. He even figures the jackrabbits is trying to steal it from him. I was glad to get outta there."

"I can see you were, Billy Joy. In fact, you seem glad to be here."

"Yes, sir."

"Why?"

She looked at me quizzically. "Can I ask you a question, first?"

"All right."

"See, when it comes to sex, I haven't any self-control at all. I'm powerless to resist. Do you think I'm oversexed?"

"No, I don't think there is any such thing," I said.

"You don't?" She seemed disappointed. "Well, my pa thinks I am. My probation officer said they should send me to some kind of clinic in Kansas that advertised they could give medicine to desex girls. If you don't believe me, I can show you the advertisement."

"I believe you," I said.

"Uncontrolled production of the hormones that control the appetite can be corrected," she quoted.

Suddenly she stood up, shuddered, and shrieked. "I don't want to go!"

"You wanted to come here instead?"

"Yes, God, yes. I asked the judge, couldn't I please come here?"

"I don't blame you," I said. "The most important thing we can do for you is to protect you from being desexed, isn't it?"

"Oh, God, I've been scared. I hope I'm safe here. Am I?"

"Yes, you are, Billy Joy. We have a good doctor here and

no honest doctor would have anything to do with an action like that. I also promise I'll do everything I can to prevent it now, or later."

"Oh, thank you. I'm sorry, I mean thank you, sir."

"Why do you apologize?"

"Because I get the back of my father's hand if I don't say 'sir.' "

"It isn't important to me, but I expect you do want to stay in practice."

"Yes, sir, I'd better, sir. Pa knocked a nigger-Indian that was working for us, flat on his ass because he didn't say, 'sir.' What am I going to do to control my sex urge when even being afraid of Pa doesn't stop me?"

"Do you want to control it?"

"Sure, it got me in this fix, didn't it?" She put her hand on her stomach.

"That doesn't really prove that you want to be different."

"Yes, sir, I see what you mean. Well, yes I do and no I don't."

"Perhaps the problem is wanting to," I said.

"Yeah. I feel possessed by the devil and I feel like he's telling me to laugh at Pa and have fun."

"Your father has something to do with it."

"If he wasn't about to kill me for it, I wouldn't have half as much fun. I might not even want to. It seems like he's making me do it and it's his fault."

"Do you think he can make you do it by forbidding you?"

"Well, he does, because he makes me feel that way."

"You seem to say you haven't any control over your feelings toward your father."

"I keep myself from killing him."

We went in more circles that ended with her father. Time here away from him would help. I was glad with Billy Joy that she had come here.

Next I was to see Jeannine Post. Mrs. Winifred explained, "She is a beautiful, sweet child, and I feel so sorry for her."

The description made me uncomfortable. I reviewed the girl's file while I waited for her.

Jeannine was the illegitimate child of a woman who placed her in an orphanage for three years, and at length released her for adoption. The toddler was then adopted by a childless minister and his wife. They subsequently became missionaries on an Indian reservation and Jeannine grew up there. She was committed to us partly at her own request, and because she had run away from home.

She was a fragile brunette with fair skin and smoke-blue eyes. The record showed her to be seventeen but she looked younger, yet fatigued of life as though the years had been long. She moved into my office slowly and hesitantly. She obviously had been sleeping.

I smiled at her. "Jeannine, I am a psychologist and my job is to help you. I hope you will let me help you."

"Everyone has been very nice to me," she said, so softly I could just hear her.

"But you don't seem very happy."

She shrugged her slight shoulders and looked bitter.

"You may tell me why you are here if you want to."

She paused before each answer as though it were difficult to summon the energy to speak. "I wanted to be on my own and it isn't legal."

"I notice that you were on your own for awhile."

"Uh huh, I had a job in a trading post and I was in an apartment with another girl for three weeks."

"What happened?"

"I turned myself in."

"You have apparently wanted to come here for a long time. More than two years ago you went to the police and asked to be committed," I said.

"Yes. It took a long time but I finally made it."

"Why did you want to come here?"

"Because I am a bad person."

"Are you really?"

"Yes, I am wicked and evil."

"How are you bad?"

"I just am. I am going to turn out bad. I bring out the evil in people. Evil begets evil."

"Do you think we can help you?" I asked.

"I don't think anyone can help. It's too late."

"But you want to be here."

"I deserve to be here, don't I?"

"For punishment?"

"Yes, because I am bad."

"You are terribly concerned about being bad, Jeannine."

"Isn't everyone?"

"No, people are concerned about many different things, like being wise, or having fun, or being kind."

"Oh yes, fleshly things."

"I see. Your parents are missionaries, aren't they?"

"Yes," she said, so flatly that I felt she wanted to avoid talking about it.

"Were you lonely sometimes?"

"Yes. Daddy wouldn't let me be friends with the Indian young people, except under supervision, unless they had been saved and baptised and confirmed in the Spirit. There wasn't anyone else except when I went to high school."

"Did you have friends in high school?"

"It took seventy-five minutes each way on the bus and I didn't have any time at school to make friends."

"You were very lonely then."

"Yes, sometimes it seemed to me there was nothing in the world but God and the wind. The wind always blew out on the high mesa."

"Did you have a boy friend, Jeannine?"

She turned pale and said, "Yes, once."

I waited. Each time she paused I waited.

"It was wrong of me but it didn't seem wrong. He was an Indian boy and we loved each other. My father said God had made us different and our love would be miscegenation. He said the Indians had been cursed and turned black and only the grace of God could save them. I couldn't understand how God could curse Roy when he was such a gentle person, or how he could curse a child that hadn't even been born yet. I questioned the holy word and that was even a bigger sin than loving Roy."

I must have allowed my unbelief to appear in my eyes because she explained. "I could be forgiven if I were truly penitent and would not do it again. But if Roy came for me, I know I would go with him, and I still don't believe God has cursed all the Indians. I try to believe it, but I can't. Even when I read Genesis 9:25 I still don't believe it."

I was trying not to listen to the theology. I tried to listen to Jeannine's feelings. She could reconstruct her own theology, but she couldn't manage her feelings alone.

"My sin makes me hate and hate is another sin," she said. "Because of me, Roy was sent to Indian School in Oklahoma, so I have caused suffering to him. My parents suffer because of me. Everyone I touch is hurt and I am an instrument of the devil."

We wordlessly shared the despair of her fall from grace. When she began to drift into reverie, I asked, "Jeannine, do you have any hobbies or special interests?"

"I play the piano," she said.

"What kind of music do you like?"

"I like a lot of kinds, but my father only likes religious music and some kinds that I like lead to temptation. No matter what kind I play, I'm possessed when I touch my hands to the keyboard. I lose all track of time. Mother taught me piano, and until the pains in her back stopped her from playing she was possessed like me." There was spirit in her eyes now and she looked at me as she talked.

"Jeannine, do you feel guilty when you play because of your father's attitude?"

"Not really. My mother understands. Music to me is neither good nor bad. It's another world, like painting and poetry."

"You paint, and write poetry?" I asked.

"I did. That's how I met Roy. We were in high school art class and he was the most talented person in the class. He painted deer in a style all his own. You may have seen horses done that way by an Indian artist named Momaday. Roy painted deer. I don't believe anyone who ever saw one of Roy's paintings could ever kill a deer again. Their eyes were so beautiful and so sensitive. They haunt me now when I think about it. Roy had eyes like that. I did some of Roy's backgrounds for him. He liked my touch with landscapes." As she finished speaking of Roy the depression returned and she seemed infinitely tired.

We rested a moment.

"Jeannine, what do you look forward to?" I asked.

She stared at the floor and then writhed in response to some thought. "Being dead," she said finally.

I stopped and took inventory of the girl. "She is slow and delayed in response," I said to myself. "She turns her hostility on herself. She wants to be punished. She wishes for death. How depressed is she? Suicidal?"

Aloud I asked, "Jeannine, are you tired very much of the time?"

"I guess I could sleep almost all the time."

"Are you tired when there is something you really want to do?"

"I don't want to do anything. I don't care about anything. I just—don't—care anymore."

"Do you sleep well?"

"Yes, except when I have bad dreams." She stared at the floor.

"Would you like to tell me what you dream about?"

"They are making me go back home and I wake up fighting, or sometimes I'm dead, and in a coffin and dressed all in white with one white lily in my hand, and suddenly the coffin moves and I wake up."

"You think quite a lot about death," I said. I was being deliberately casual, suppressing my compassion.

"Lately I do," she said.

"Have you ever tried to kill yourself?"

"Not yet."

I became firm now, almost severe. "Jeannine, I want you to give me a chance to help you. I want to see you every day and if you feel you can't stand it at night, I want you to have the housemother call me. I am going to call the medical doctor, and ask him to give you some medicine. You be sure to take it. It will help."

She was startled at the change in my manner. "Yes, sir." She straightened a little.

"When do they give you your clothes?" I asked.

"Tomorrow."

"Good, you won't have to talk to me tomorrow in this nightgown."

She clutched at it and I said, "Now, will you be all right until tomorrow morning?"

"Yes, sir—I think so."

When Jeannine left, I followed, and I watched Mrs. Winifred bustle up, hug her, and tell her what a sweet girl she was. The girl shook her head in protest and collapsed into self-contempt once more.

"Damn it," I said. With guilt like that, unearned praise would make her feel more guilty.

I called Dr. Norden, the M.D., and discussed Jeannine with him. He had recognized the depression, too, and had debated whether she should be sent to the State Hospital, but decided that we could send her later if close observation indicated the need. He said he would prescribe an ample dose of antidepressant, and I felt relieved. We both lamented that no psychiatric consultant was available, but by working together we felt we could help the girl.

I needed Mrs. Winifred's help, not her judgment this time, and I wanted her to follow directions. When she returned, I stood up and spoke to her as I would to a nurse under these circumstances. "Mrs. Winifred, Jeannine is ill. She is seriously depressed, consumed with guilt, and possibly suicidal."

Mrs. Winifred gasped a little.

"She must be watched closely, and she must be treated in a carefully casual way. You are a kind and motherly person, and it may be hard for you, but she must be treated casually and even a little brusquely."

"I thought I should be nice to all the girls," she said.

"Ordinarily, yes. This is different. Every bit of anger this girl feels is turned against herself. She thinks she is a very wicked person, and when anyone is too nice to her, it deepens her guilt. If she feels too guilty, she may destroy herself."

"Well, how should I act?"

"Just businesslike."

"Well, I'll try, Doctor, but this is certainly new to me. All my life I've worked with young people and I never—but you know best." She shrugged.

"If she asks to see me at any time, night or day, you must call me," I said.

I didn't mind frightening the housemother about this. A

profound depression is an emergency, and I would be apprehensive until it lifted, remembering how Jeannine had responded about suicide with, "Not yet."

On return to my office, I found Marsha Mabry waiting for me, notebook and pencil in hand. She looked vibrant and purposeful.

"What's on your mind, Marsha?"

"I want to interview you for my English assignment. It's about careers. I've decided something. I hope you won't laugh, because I really mean it, and I know I can do it."

"You know that I won't laugh," I said.

"I've decided to become a psychologist. I think I might have some talent for it because lately the other girls have been talking to me about their problems, and I really do want to help people."

"I'm sure you can become a good psychologist, Marsha."

"What do I have to do? How do I go about it? I know it takes a lot of education." She spoke eagerly and waved her notebook.

Now that Marsha identified so much with me, so much as to model herself after me, there was little doubt that the changes in her would be profound and lasting. This was, perhaps, evidence of "transference." I smiled to think how new therapists and patients alike shrank from the spector of transference, envisioning a struggle of countertransferences and compulsions on both sides like wrestling with the devil. It was not like that at all. It merely meant I must wait with constant fatherly concern while Marsha outgrew her need for me. Right now, she needed to know how to become a psychologist.

I had finished my discourse and she was at the door when she changed the subject. "There is something else I need to know about," she said. "How should a girl go about ducking a pass?"

"How do you do it, Marsha?"

"I haven't had much practice except with young boys. Them, I just bat in the teeth. Last weekend my English teacher, Mrs. Brainerd, had me over to her house. I was doing the dishes and she went grocery shopping, so her brother, he's about thirty-five years old, was there in the house. He came in the kitchen and sat down in the chair near me and warmed up to me. He was getting fresher all the time and I stopped talking and scrubbed on the pans. Then he said he liked the way I was stacked and he reached over and took hold of my leg. I didn't know what to do."

"What did you do?"

"I took a big dish pan of water and I threw it in his lap," she said.

"I'll bet that stopped him."

"Yeah, it sure did, but there must be an easier way, more ladylike."

"I guess I can't qualify as an expert on that subject, Marsha. Would you like to talk to Miss Swanson about it?"

I took her to Miss Swanson's office and explained our mission.

"Doctor, you are so flattering," said Miss Swanson. "I'll help all I can," she said, and excused me.

Miss Swanson came to tell me about it thirty minutes later. "You know," she said, "it makes me so furious. Almost invariably when one of our girls goes out to a home, some chauvinistic male makes a crude pass at her. They seem to think that being sentenced here has labeled any girl fair and willing game."

"I suppose sometimes they are," I said.

"Yes, but more often, they aren't," she said. "Marsha gave that fool absolutely no encouragement. I told her to be cautious about little flirtations that get out of hand, but she knew all about that."

"The defense pleads guilty and throws itself on the mercy of the court," I said.

"Oh, I'm sorry. I know you aren't responsible for all the beastly men in the world." she said.

VIII

Group therapy could help my girls in some ways I couldn't help otherwise. I began as usual with discomfort about it. In our culture the tender feelings have grown to be private and tough ones public, so that group therapy often begins at the lowest common denominator of feelings. Nevertheless, we needed growth at that level too, and we had time to wait for tenderness.

I wanted Saralee in the group because she needed friends and stayed too much alone in her homesick funk. Jeannine, too was lonely because she had lived so long in the isolation of the reservation mission and felt herself a stranger with the other girls. Marsha could contribute constructively to the group. Billy Joy needed awareness of a cultural world other than her own, and Frances needed to think about her own life and values, rather than merely reacting to the estrangement of her parents.

We met around the conference table in the board room. It would have been better in a more informal setting. The girls reacted at first with awe. Saralee and Franny sat close together and whispered to each other. Billy Joy crocheted clumsily on a blue baby garment while Jeannine and Marsha watched her.

I felt awkward while I explained what we were going to do, so I said I felt awkward and that they probably did too.

Complete freedom of speech usually inhibits the opening of conversation.

"Is this where the board meets?" asked Billy Joy, without looking up.

"That's right," I said.

"Mr. Chairman, I demand a pass. No, I mean, I demand a parole."

"Who wants to be chairman of the board?" I asked.

"I will," said Marsha. "You're out of order, Billy Joy."

"I'm always out of order. I demand a parole." Billy Joy abandoned her snarled handiwork and banged on the table.

"Request refused," said Marsha. "Come back in two years and keep your nose clean."

Billy Joy flared up. "My nose is cleaner now than it will be then, and you know it. I make a motion we put the chairman in lock. All in favor say aye."

"Aye!" they all yelled, and all but Jeannine were on their feet pushing Marsha into a corner. Marsha dropped out of character to escape injury.

When the uproar subsided, I said that everyone wished they had power, like a chairman or a judge or a policeman has.

"Yeah," said Franny. "Everyone has power but kids."

"People use it too," said Saralee, "pushing kids around, pushing and pushing and pushing us around."

"Like my probation officer said, I wasn't going to blow my nose without permission from him," Frances said, and blew her nose loudly.

"What gets me," said Marsha, "is the hypocrisy. They sent up a boy I know for driving drunk because they found three empty beer cans in his car. Man, you could arrest 5000 drunk driving adults every night just by parking outside the bars."

"It isn't what you do, it's who you are," Saralee said.

"That's true," Marsha agreed. "I know two boys that broke into a liquor store. The guy from a poor family got sent up and the doctor's son got sent to live with his uncle for three months."

"Yeah, or like I came here because I'm pregnant and Miss Fancy Jeans gets an abortion." Billy Joy checked the development of her stomach.

"Are you going to have a baby?" asked Jeannine.

"Yeah," said Billy Joy, picking up her crocheting, "by my preacher—or my teacher—I ain't sure which."

Jeannine reacted with shock and withdrew.

"There you are again," said Marsha. "I'll bet the preacher and the teacher aren't in jail."

"Are you kidding? Of course they aren't. They're men," Billy Joy said.

"Men can get away with anything," Frances said. "I wish I was a man."

"Who doesn't?" asked Billy Joy.

"Ladies don't do this and ladies don't do that," Saralee said.

Billy Joy was getting more expansive. "Yeah, but a boy can whore around all over the country and it makes him a big man. A girl has some fun just once and it makes her a . . ."

"A tramp," said Franny.

"Or even if she doesn't, some bastard brags that he made you, and you have to claw up three or four guys before you live it down," Marsha said.

"I hate men!" Billy Joy said. "I wish they weren't necessary."

"I'm never going to get married," Saralee said.

"I wish I weren't going to," Frances said.

Jeannine said, "I'm not."

There was a pause and I said, "You feel that marriage is painful and unhappy, and being a married woman is nothing to look forward to."

"After a woman has a baby and a husband," Marsha said,

"she does about six times as much work as a man does."

"And then gets beat up on Saturday night," added Saralee.

"No son of a bitch is ever going to beat up on me." Billy Joy stabbed the table with the crochet hook.

Marsha said, "I'd like to meet a boy just once that didn't have the same dirty thing on his mind."

"Don't be dumb," said Frances. "There isn't any boy like that. Sex, sex, sex, that's all they can think of."

"Yes, and when they knock you up, they think it makes them big men. I wish I could have my babies without a man," Saralee said.

"You can," Billy Joy said. "A doctor can do artificial insemination just like they do with cows."

"Yeah?"

"Sure. One bull can handle I don't know how many cows that way."

"Ugh. It sounds even dirtier that way," said Saralee.

"Well, it don't appeal to me exactly," Billy Joy said. "To tell the truth, I think sex is fun. I just don't want to get married."

Frances and Saralee looked at each other and giggled.

"You have a point," said Marsha. "I'm interested in sex too, but I don't like the consequences."

Encouraged by the others, Frances confessed, "What I like to do is get a guy all worked up and then leave him standing there with a stone ache. That's funny. They look so funny, all hung up."

"That's mean," said Saralee.

"Yeah, but it's funny," Franny said through her laughter.

"It may be funny, Fran, but it's dangerous," Marsha told her. "Some guy might rape you."

"Men hurt women, so women want to hurt men," I said.

"But women are hurt more, aren't they?" Marsha asked.

"I guess so, Marsha."

"You damn right they are," Billy Joy said to me. "Do you know any men that have babies?"

"Or have the curse every month?" asked Frances.

"Or did you ever hear of a man that got up at night and changed diapers?" asked Saralee. "They don't even stay home."

"No. They're off fishing or hunting or breaking horses." Billy Joy was on her feet strutting around in imitation of men. "Or maybe they are off drag-racing or having a beer or making some broad."

They all looked at me, waiting for an answer.

"I apologize for men," I said.

They were shocked into silence by my apology.

"We didn't mean to be mean to you," said Saralee.

"Maybe it doesn't have to be the way we said it was," Marsha said.

Jeannine spoke clearly now, "It could be so nice if people would just be kind to each other."

I wanted to respond to Jeannine, to re-enforce so she would take part again. "Yes, Jeannine, it seems a shame to have the men against women and the women against men, doesn't it."

This was catharsis moving at breakneck speed and I reviewed in my mind what had happened. They shared their terrible hostility towards adults and toward men. They had revealed their rejection of being women with all that womanhood involved, including marriage. Motherhood, they did not fully reject. Coitus they regarded as dirty, but admitted it was exciting. Jeannine was unable to share the catharsis. Marsha and Jeannine were either sparing my feelings or had some concept of another kind of male-female relationship. I represented to the group an adult and a man, and I was being belabored for it. I could tell them my feelings, some of them.

"I am an adult and a man and I am part of the legal system. That's why you are giving me a bad time," I said.

"Who else can we give a bad time?" asked Billy Joy.

"I'm glad you are. If you feel that way about it, I want to understand. Thanks for telling me."

"Now that I said all that, I feel ashamed," Marsha said.

"For Christ sake why?" asked Billy Joy. "I ain't said half of what I'd like to say."

"You're madder than I am," Marsha said.

"You ain't pregnant," Billy Joy said. "I've got a bellyfull."

Franny laughed.

"I wanted my baby," said Saralee. "How can you be mean to a little baby?"

"Yes," said Jeannine.

Billy Joy smouldered.

I said, "Billy Joy didn't say she felt mean towards the baby. She said, I think, that she felt mean about being pregnant."

"I guess I just feel mean," said Billy Joy.

"So do I sometimes," Marsha said, "especially before my period and on the first day, I hate everything and mostly I hate myself."

"You feel that way?" asked Jeannine. "I hate myself all the time."

Frances was serious now. "I don't exactly hate myself, but I want to hurt myself. See those?" She showed three long scratches on her neck. "I did that to myself."

Saralee had her thumb nail in her mouth and whimpered.

"Hate is awful, isn't it? How can you stop hating?" Marsha asked me.

"I don't know if you can stop hating. Everyone feels hatred sometimes. I think it's more a question of what you do with it."

"Yeah, like who do you kill," said Billy Joy. "What else can you do with it?"

"I feel better when I talk about it," said Marsha.

"When I go home, I don't hate anybody," said Saralee.

"When you get away from your problem, it gets easier," said Jeannine.

They were each on their own train of thought. "You each have different problems and when the problem gets better you feel better and hate less," I said.

"What can we do about a problem in here?" asked Saralee.

"All you can do is sit and wait," said Billy Joy.

Franny laughed sardonically and threw her hand in the air. "We're right back where we started. The adults have all the power. See?"

Even Jeannine smiled.

"I don't think that's so," Marsha said. "You can straighten out your own thinking. When I came here I was trying to make my parents change. I wasn't trying to get along. I was so mad at them that all I could think of was to do any fool thing that would make them stop fighting, or get somebody else to make them stop. When I got here there wasn't much to be mad about and I had time to think. I've decided now I can't make them stop fighting. That's their problem. What I can do something about is me. Nothing changed at all, I guess, except me."

The others were interested but didn't respond.

"The way you looked at the problem made a difference, Marsha?" I asked.

"Yeah, and talking about it, too. You made me think better."

"I don't want to think any better about being away from my mother and my baby," said Saralee.

"That's up to you," said Marsha.

"People keep telling me how I'm supposed to feel. I want to feel the way I feel," Saralee said.

"We'll try not to tell you how you're supposed to feel,

Saralee. We'll try to understand how you really do feel," I said.

"That's one thing they can't boss you about. They can't make you change your feelings," Billy Joy said.

"That's right," I said. "I can't make you change your feelings; the judge can't; nobody can."

"I was afraid they could," said Franny, "but I wasn't going to let them."

"I guess that's a power we have," said Marsha.

"Thank God and amen," said Billy Joy.

That seemed a strategic place to close the meeting, I thought. I closed, assuring them that one more power they had was to come, or not to come, to this group.

IX

The coming board meeting required a decision. I could be conciliatory and keep the peace, or I could involve the board in the real issues and bring some changes, good or bad. My decision to forget discretion was not a judgment at all, but simply a surrender to my own disposition. I liked conflict, especially intellectual conflict, and I liked being a missionary for my profession. More than that, there was always the hope that out of conflict would come a creative meeting of minds, a real resolution, and a fresh, cooperative approach.

Facing a self-created conflict with them, I felt apprehensive, but eager. When I arrived, Miss Loomis was taking the lead, I was pleased to note. She was securing their approval for paroles, trial visits, and earned privilege passes. Among them were the trial visit for Saralee Austin and the earned privilege pass for Marsha Mabry. In both cases, Miss Loomis appended to her request the remark, "This has not yet been cleared with the district court so the board's approval will take effect only after approval of the court." Both requests, like the others, were approved perfunctorily. The board seemed acquiescent. I hoped that meant receptive.

Mr. Woolman made a place for me at the table and said, "The floor is for you, Doctor."

"I haven't seen you all week, Doctor," said Lola Kittredge, extending her hand to me in a way that suggested she was expecting a courtly hand kiss. I disappointed her.

Mrs. Purdy appeared to already disagree with what I would say, and I would certainly not disappoint her by withholding my thoughts. I spoke from very detailed notes but knew them well enough so that I could watch my audience.

"Thank you, Mr. Woolman. One of the satisfactions of labor is working with other good people and sharing thoughts about how we can improve our work. Just as I appreciate Miss Loomis and the other staff people I am working with, I also value talking with you about the great responsibility that we share. I say 'talking with you' rather than 'talking to you' because I hope you will react to what I say. I want the stimulation you can give me to modify and refine my thinking. I want to learn from your ideas, and I hope that we can arrive eventually at a common point of view which will be more complete, more correct, and more practical because we have all contributed to it."

I had planned that I would first open the door to their minds, continue by getting their involvement, and persuade at the end when I had them ready. Seeing the three women braced against me, I was happy I had planned that approach.

"I want to open with several observations about this institution. The first is that the sensible routine of life here, the good food, the good medical care, the good dental care, the exercise, and the help in grooming, all have a salutary effect upon these girls, especially upon those from impoverished and chaotic backgrounds."

It was evident that I had every board member in agreement. "Secondly, I wish to observe that I feel well prepared to work with these girls but I have a great deal to learn about working in this setting. The fact that these girls are sentenced here by the court and confined here under these particular conditions creates a whole set of circumstances different from any I have worked in before. I am learning from the staff how to work with the district courts and with the other structures and procedures necessary to the operation of this institution.

"Thirdly, I wish to observe that the authority of each of the nine district courts extends into this institution. Each judge is in a position to prescribe specific programs and restrictions upon our programs. Similarly the authority of this institution extends into the jurisdictional area of the courts. Miss Loomis has the impossible task of being responsible to ten employers, this board and nine judges. I know little of law and little about administration, but I do know what conditions are conducive to professional work. I think that some careful study is needed to establish clear cut lines of authority and responsibility. What do you people think?"

Bishop Elder said, "We have found the situation you describe to be confusing and difficult. Recently we debated establishing a minimum sentence for the girls. We were not sure that it was the best thing to do, but the issue was dropped because we decided we had no authority to make such a decision."

"I think this really should come to the attention of the governor," Mrs. Kittredge said. "I would be happy to go to him with it."

"What now happens," Miss Loomis said, "is that we veto each other. For example, when we think a girl is ready for a visit home, or discharge, the court may veto the idea. Or, if the court makes the same decision, we may veto the idea. It will not be an easy issue to resolve but we ought to try."

After some discussion it was agreed that Bishop Elder and Mrs. Kittredge and Miss Loomis would proceed to seek guidance from the governor. At the suggestion of Miss Loomis it was agreed that she would prepare a list of typical problems that arose from the confused jurisdiction.

Mrs. Purdy and Mrs. Kittredge had relaxed. My beach head was established. When they concluded their planning on that issue, I began speaking quietly. "I would like to present to you now a number of facts and a few conclusions about the girls.

"More than half of the girls come from broken homes. Many of their mothers have married repeatedly. One girl's mother has been married ten times. That is not quite as bad as it sounds because she married one of the men twice. In some additional cases where no divorce is involved, the father long ago deserted the family. In a few cases a girl has never known a father, merely a succession of men visitors in the home. The girl with an intact home is an exception here.

"Alcoholism is common in these families. Talking with Nancy, one of the new girls, the other day, I asked 'What is it like at home?' Her response was, 'Oh, I come from a regular average home like everybody else, I guess. My father is an alcoholic.'

"Many of the girls, perhaps as many as twenty-five percent, experienced incestuous relationships with their father, stepfather, uncle, or brother before they were twelve years of age. In poor working class families, or welfare level families, when incest occurs the blame is often placed on the little girl. It is common among many of these families to view all men as sexually irresponsible, so the girl child is blamed. Furthermore, the wife is often too afraid of a brutal husband to confront him, so she can only solve the problem by sending the girl out of the home."

Mrs. Purdy was stiffening a little as I talked, but she was interested.

"Around twenty percent of our girls have one or two parents who have been to the State Hospital for psychiatric reasons and several of our girls have a parent there now. Almost half of them have had some member of the family in the state penitentiary, and six girls have fathers presently in prison in this state or elsewhere.

"Some of the girls have less measurably pathological environments, but I have yet to identify one family where there was not a substantial problem. Each situation is difficult. In one, a mother accuses all her girl children of sexual misbehavior from the time they are five years old. In another, the mother actually sells her girl children to men. In some, the father regularly beats and rapes his wife in the hearing of the children.

"Perhaps I have said enough to make it evident that these are not merely homes with problems. These are destructive environments."

"Have you any observations about the religious life in these homes?" asked the bishop.

"Yes, it is evident that these families seldom belong actively to any church group, or any other social group. They are non-belongers in their own communities; so are the girls. The girls have belonged to no clubs or organizations of any kind and were never in extracurricular activities, nor organized recreational activities. There are exceptions to everything I say here, but they are, as they say, exceptions that prove the point.

"The girls themselves have certain characteristics. When you make allowances for their poor cultural background, they are above average in intelligence. There are many who are intellectually bright and even a few who are gifted. Among the duller ones there is often a social shrewdness, a manual dexterity, musical or athletic talents that are impressive. They are healthy in spite of poor diets.

"In spite of these abilities they have developed almost no effective skills for happy living. Few of them know how to cook, sew, paint, sing, dance, dress, act, converse, or play games of any kind. Their school attendance has been so poor that they perform in school far below their potential. They know how to read but have read almost nothing of value.

"What these girls do know how to do is fight. They are aggressive personalities, strong personalities. They did not drift into delinquency; they exploded into it. When other teenagers drank their beer furtively, these did it openly and defiantly. One of the girls told me that one of the charges against her was throwing her empty beer can into a police car—with the policeman in it. Another girl stole a police car from in front of the police station at high noon. I am sure all of you have heard the story of the girl who two years ago broke out of here, hitchhiked directly to the state capital, and was caught when she broke into the governor's mansion.

"Frequently, they made no attempt to conceal their delinquency. They were protestors. Sometimes they knew exactly what they were protesting against just as the Boston tea partiers did, but more often they staged a blind, straw grasping, raging protest against their environment.

"By the time they came here these girls had a well developed poor opinion of themselves. They often respond here initially with a good adjustment, because they have capacity for it. We sometimes wonder for a few days why a girl is here. Presently she tells us in very plain behavior, sometimes plain language. She knows how to fight better than she knows how to adjust. They often say outright, 'I am a bad girl so I am going to act like one.' They grew for various reasons to feel they were worthless, stupid, ugly and bad, so they try to win distinction by being the worst of human beings, having lost hope of ever being good at anything.

"Mother Reed, who is quite a remarkable housemother, was telling me about something she overheard. Two of the younger girls were playing games of pretend in the day room and she heard one of them say, 'I know what. Let's pretend we're good.' "

I could see I had scored with that story. The bishop lifted his glasses and wiped under them; Lola looked down at her hands folded in her lap; the rest seemed visibly shaken. I continued.

"In the first few weeks here, many of the girls proceed to show us how bad they can be. They boast of their delinquency, attempt escape, fight, curse, tattoo themselves, and test every rule. Some of them protest with hunger strikes, or suicide attempts. They probably behave much worse than they have ever behaved before because they have now been labeled as one of the one-hundred-fifty-most-delinquent-girls in the state. This period of anger is familiar to most people who have worked with deeply angry adults or children. If the anger is not recreated it tends to play itself out in about three months.

"During the whole period preceding the sentencing and through this first three months, they truly do not care about themselves, nor anyone else for that matter. Many people try to persuade them to behave differently by pointing out how they are hurting themselves, assuming that they care, or trying to convince them they should care. It is not productive. What is productive is to listen to them tell why they don't care. They explain quite eloquently. They don't feel cared about.

"One girl was boasting to me about how she came home drunk and with her boy friend at two o'clock in the morning. I asked what her mother had done about it. She said, 'Oh, my mother didn't care enough about me to do anything.'

"They also don't care about themselves because their anger is so overwhelming that they can feel nothing else.

"As staff, we can do little to help during this long period but listen, and understand, and control them with as little punishment as possible and as much caring about them as we can muster. We can not help them until they want our help, and they cannot want our help until they trust us. We work very hard to win their trust."

I saw the first signs of restlessness in the women now and decided it was time to stop talking.

"There is another story to tell you about the changes that take place in these girls, and how they are brought about, but I think that might be told another time. I would like now to hear your response and reaction to my description of the girls."

It was Mrs. Purdy, of course, who challenged me. "Doctor, you have described delinquency as a purposeful protest. Don't you believe children sometimes misbehave simply because they can get away with it? And for that matter, isn't it natural human frailty to indulge the basic appetites unless they are curbed?"

"You feel that children are just naturally delinquent, Mrs. Purdy?"

"I think that every child does what he wants to do, makes his own rules, and violates society's rules unless he has good reason to do otherwise. In fact, I have observed very young children, uncontrolled by their parents, do outrageous things."

"That is a very good point, Mrs. Purdy. If I gave the impression that I think all children are naturally well behaved, except when corrupted by society, I didn't mean to do so."

"I should hope not." she said.

"One phrase you used, Mrs. Purdy, seems to me the key idea," I said. "Children become civilized when they have a good reason to. Well-behaved children feel cared for, and cared about, profoundly and personally, possibly cared enough about to be spanked as well as loved. Delinquent children don't feel cared about, and as a result don't care about themselves."

"You strongly suggest that you don't believe punishment is a deterrent," she said.

"Mrs. Purdy, I flatly believe that punishment without love is not a deterrent. In fact, I believe that punishment without love provokes delinquency."

Bishop Elder had an urgent thought. "If that is true, and I am inclined to believe it is, then perhaps this institution shouldn't exist. The punishment of being sent here is not apt to be understood as an act of love."

"Good heavens, Bishop Elder," Mabel Anderson said with wide, frightened eyes, "if there weren't any reformatory the delinquents would take over the state." Everyone laughed but Mrs. Purdy.

"Mrs. Anderson," I said, "that, I am sure, is what almost everyone thinks. The penal institutions have a very important role in our society because they are the final threat of exile. We have a lingering idea from our puritan heritage that an overwhelming evil lurks in each of us and the threat of death or exile is a finger in the dike—the only thing that prevents a deluge of crime from destroying us all. Even more so, I suppose, the electric chair and that bird cage down in the basement are the ultimate threats, as some people see it, the final bulwark against chaos and debauchery. I question the concept of prevention by threat. Exactly the opposite may be true. Almost every girl I have talked with here wanted to come. The threat of being sent here ultimately made them want to be here."

I hoped earlier that I had dented Mrs. Purdy's armor of disbelief, but she was regrouping her ideas and assailing me with them, alert to every opportunity to discredit my position. "Again you suggest," she said, "that you would do away with confinement and let delinquency go unchallenged."

"Mrs. Purdy, that is not my position, but you make me realize that I must propose an alternative. First, about confinement, many penologists estimate that eighty-five percent of offenders could be rehabilitated in their own community, more cheaply and effectively than by serving a prison term first and then rehabilitating, or suffering repeat performances in prison. I would not, if I could, release eighty-five percent of the girls from this institution in the near future. I would, if I could, establish skilled help in each community and move in the direction of rehabilitation rather than confinement. I would move that way as rapidly as I could make it work effectively."

Now Mrs. Kittredge was alarmed. "Well, that would make this a very small institution, with all the investment in buildings going to waste."

"Possibly so, Mrs. Kittredge," I said. "Mrs. Purdy, the other thing you suspected from my words was that delinquency might go unchallenged. I object to that. I would challenge it promptly and repeatedly and forthrightly. I would confront every instance of delinquency and examine all the causes of it. I would expect the child to be more responsible, the parents to be more responsible, and the whole community to be more responsible. Without going into detail about many things I would do—things that are being done in some communities—let me assure you that you and I are in accord in believing that delinquency must be challenged. I only question the system of challenge which does nothing but exile the child."

"Would the family court be one of the community approaches?" Bishop Elder asked.

As he spoke, Mrs. Purdy and Mrs. Kittredge huddled to exchange ideas and the discussion broke up into smaller groups, each group heatedly involved.

I took the opportunity to tell Bishop Elder about Jeannine and how her father's theology doomed her to guilt and depression. We discussed together how a gradual exposure to another religious outlook might help her. He agreed that abrupt argument might only intensify her guilt. I left it in his hands to plan with the chaplain an approach, probably through her music.

Turning to Miss Loomis, I expressed again the satisfaction that I always felt in working with the

Presently, I became aware that the bishop and Mr.
man had gone. Lola Kittredge and Mabel Anderson were s
ing near the door.

As I said good night to Mrs. Purdy and Miss Loomis, I
pulled my professional manner more tightly around me and
moved to the door where the other two women waited. Mabel
Anderson stepped out first, then Lola Kittredge, who held the
door open for me.

"Thank you, Mrs. Kittredge," I said.

"Oh, Doctor, you are so formal," she said. She was working her hands nervously. "Doctor, your speech was just beautiful but something you said distressed me terribly. Everything
I have planned may be changed by what you said about the
home growing smaller. How about discussing it with us over
a drink?"

"Thank you, but it's really quite late."

The women had maneuvered until I was walking between
them. As we stepped into the parking area, a red Chrysler
backed out of a space at the end and wheeled up beside us.
The door swung open and the dome light shone on a beefy,
red-faced man.

"Hi, Babe!" the man yelled at Lola.

"Fats!" she said. "I told you I came with Mabel and I'd
go home with Mabel. We're going to stop for a drink. Where
is the baby?"

"He's at home asleep, Babe, you know . . ."

"Yes, I know," she said through her teeth. "Alone."

He looked down, lip out.

"Well, don't just sit there. Go on home." She spoke gaily
to Mabel as Fats drove off, "Fats is a nice enough guy. He just
gets carried away."

Mabel laughed and hitched up her brassiere. "I couldn't
talk to my husband that way."

"How about that drink, Doctor? I expect you could use one after talking to an illiterate group like we." Lola made "illiterate" a seductive word by drawling and accenting the second syllable with her hip.

I was not socially adept, and I knew it. I had seen this coming and I had grown more and more uncomfortable. The further I got into a situation like this, the less control of it I would have. I began to perspire. "Thank you, but there's a girl in the reception unit who may be suicidal and I must go and check on her."

"Oh, that won't take long," Lola said. "We'll wait."

"It's nice of you and I'd like to, but . . ." I was getting firm but she was too fast for me.

"Then you will, of course." She spoke hoarsely and tightened her fingernails on my arm. "I realize, Doctor, it won't be very intellectual company. I'm just a ranch girl as you know, but you and I are in a position to be helpful to each other and I can't imagine why you wouldn't want to. I think we should play ball with each other."

"I would like very much to talk with you again, Mrs. Kittredge. Could you come again to my office some time soon?" I knew I was stammering.

"Yes, I'll make a formal appointment, if I still need you," she said. "We shall see you later."

"Good night," I called to them as they stalked away.

I heard Mabel Anderson say, "Now that was nerve," and I heard Lola whisper back, "Shut up, Mabel."

My depressed patient was sleeping. I drove home to Bonnie more than a little depressed myself.

Although it was unpleasant to do so, a little like Napoleon pausing in Moscow to contemplate his position, I felt it was necessary now to review my dilemma.

I was in the middle of treatment with a dozen girls, consultant in the treatment of a dozen others, and assuming a role in the milieu treatment of many more. I knew I was becoming an accepted leader of the staff, a leaven by insistent respect for the personality of each child and each staff member, but also I was becoming a policy maker through my influence on Miss Loomis, not so much by persuasion as by questioning. I wanted to know, as I had been trained, how every procedure was justified and whether the purpose of rehabilitation was best served each step of the way. I was convinced that there was movement and direction, and I was committed to go on.

Yet, the faster the movement and the surer the direction, the more ominous were the conflicts and the more impending the collision because the power sources were being challenged. The board was certainly not committed to this new direction. Mrs. Purdy and Mrs. Kittredge each pressed their own personal goals, dominating the board by means of a curious alliance with each other. There was only Bishop Elder to defend our new developments; how effectively, I could not tell.

Nine judicial districts with their judges and probation officers multiplied the power sources, each braced to fight encroachment on its dukedom, each in need of the Home as its place for exile of delinquents. Considering the personalities and the passion with which their vested interests might be defended, I knew now an open conflict which might unite these power sources could be disastrous. Until the governor, and the legislature, and the public were educated and aroused, an open confrontation would certainly mean defeat and regression. From now on, I decided, the struggle must be by attrition; one probation officer, one judge, and one board member at a time.

Since I was no strategist, and certainly no diplomat, as the recent board meeting had proven, and I had no appetite for administration, I was happy to go on as I had, unraveling with each child her dilemma, educating the staff one by one, looking at policies in the light of each child, and influencing the board and the courts child by child. That was to be my contribution.

I would not seek another confrontation. If a big one came, it would come.

$$X$$

Miss Loomis asked me to interview a new fourteen-year-old named Rene Barbour, who came from the city and had created some kind of a stir among half of the agencies and officials. It was not possible from the concerned telephone calls that came in, Miss Loomis said, to tell why Rene was of such importance, but her importance was evident. After most children were confined, the community promptly relaxed its concern; but some tension remained about Rene, and I agreed to explore the situation.

Rene had that sturdy, athletic appearance one can see in any high school girls' physical education class, and did not appear sexually precocious. However, she was aggressive and impertinent.

"What do you want?" she asked me.

"I'm the psychologist."

"Oh, yeah. The head shrinker. What next?" She was still standing. She deliberately lifted the reception nightgown up around her waist and sat down, hips and panties exposed.

"Apparently you want me to see you naked," I said.

"Sure—go ahead and look."

"Why?" I asked.

"You're a man aren't you?" she said.

"I don't think you like men."

"I think they stink."

"Some man must have hurt you pretty badly."

She knit her brows and studied me as she pulled down the nightgown. "Have you met my mother?"

"No. Should I?"

"I want you to meet my mother. She'll be here this afternoon to bring my things. I'm moving down to a regular cottage right after lunch."

"Good. I'll see your mother then, if you want me to."

She stood up and said, "I want to be with her when you talk to her."

I explained carefully. "You may introduce us, and then wait while I talk with her alone."

"I'm going to be there when you talk to her," she said.

"Nope," I said.

"Then I won't ever talk to you anymore."

"That's up to you. You don't have to."

"O.K. Good-by!" she said, and slammed the door.

I was sure I would see her again soon, but I would have no information for Miss Loomis until Rene was ready.

In the afternoon I received word that Rene was with her mother in the waiting room and that she was asking to see me.

I greeted Rene casually, and as I was introduced to her mother, I remembered that I had seen her before. She had a voluptuous, European look, and an accent, but I couldn't tie her immediately to a time or place.

Rene made a determined movement to join us in my office, so I stopped and waited uncompromisingly until she retreated to a chair. Then I recalled where I had seen Mrs. Barbour. She was the mysterious woman who was with Lieutenant Governor Brice Foley in the Rathskeller.

She appraised me with a steady, shrewd look. I indicated I needed information in order to understand and help Rene.

"What do you wish to know?" she said in her slight accent. I thought it was French.

"All about Rene and why she is here."

"Rene is a very stubborn girl. She will pay no attention to me."

"Why, do you think?"

"She is very angry with me. She does not approve of me. She is young and does not understand. I have protected her from poverty and she does not know how difficult it is to live. She is ashamed of me, and I think she gets even by making big scenes with the police."

"She tries to appear very tough," I said.

"Oh, tough, yes, very tough."

"Much of it is show?"

"I have taught her to be good. She has been confirmed and she has gone to Mass as she should. She is not so bad, but she acts very drunk on one beer and curses the policemen very loud."

Mrs. Barbour went on to explain that her husband had inherited money but had squandered and mismanaged it until it was gone, and had not provided for the family since.

"Since he is gone, I am not proud of my life, Doctor, but it is the best I can do." She shrugged her shoulders with European resignation. "Will Rene be better here?"

"We will do our best to help her. How do you feel about her commitment?"

"These things are decided by others more important than I. I must do what they say. I confess I hope Rene will learn she is a child. Never has she learned she is a child. So headstrong."

"You speak as though she had been a problem all her life."

"She was, Doctor, always. Always Rene had her way."

"So you feel she is spoiled," I said.

"More than spoiled. She is too strong. She is afraid of nothing, and one must be sometimes afraid."

"I think you admire her strength," I said, still hoping that she would break through these generalities and confront Lola's problems.

She continued to evade confronting the problem with me. "Yes, she has courage. Foolish courage. She must learn to live with the world."

I felt now that she was not going to be honest, so I terminated the interview and we returned to the waiting room. As Mrs. Barbour and I approached Rene, the child looked intently at me, at her mother, and then back at me. It occurred to me that Rene had expected me to be overwhelmed by her mother's charms.

"I will be available if either of you feel I can help," I said, and left them together. I was determined to wait until I was needed.

Meanwhile I was uncomfortable about the way the world had shrunk around me with Brice Foley's mistress here in my office and his sister Lola on the board. It was difficult to suspend an opinion about Rene's importance.

I was about to leave work when the telephone switchboard operator called me. "There's an emergency in Jackson cottage," she said. "Marsha Mabry is beating up some girl." It was hard to believe.

I drove to the cottage in haste and the housemother met me at the door. "Both girls are locked in their rooms now," she puffed, "but Marsha went berserk. I thought she was going to tear the new girl to pieces."

"What new girl?"

"Rene Barbour."

"Let me talk to Marsha alone," I said.

"Marsha has been doing so beautifully," said the housemother as she seated me. "I just can't imagine what possessed her."

Marsha entered the room defensively and stood waiting. "Have a seat Marsha," I said. "Let's talk a minute." The housemother left the room. Marsha sat down and said nothing.

"Do you want to tell me about it?" I asked.

"No." She tightened her lips and braced against my persuasion so obviously that I chuckled.

"It isn't funny," she said.

"I suppose it wasn't funny—whatever made you so angry at Rene."

"I'll do it again if she says it again."

"It must have been an awful thing she said."

She looked wisely at me, recognizing my technique.

"I'm not going to tell you," she said.

"Look, Marsha, maybe you shouldn't tell me. I don't know. But I think you are underestimating my ability to handle this situation. Besides, Rene is my patient, too, and I may need to know about it to help her."

Marsha thought about it for a minute. "Well, she called you a terrible name, probably the worst thing she could say."

I spoke carefully, thinking as I spoke, "My feelings about that are mixed, Marsha. I'm not at all bothered about Rene calling me a name, but I am concerned that your feelings are upset about it. I don't want you to be in trouble for defending me. I don't honestly feel I need you to defend me against Rene. I'm flattered that you want to, but I can't see the need."

"You don't know what she called you."

"No, I don't, but I don't think that changes it."

"She called you a queer," she said, "a homosexual."

I was dumbfounded for a moment. Why would Rene think that? I could think of nothing I had said or done which could be misunderstood. Then I remembered the look she gave me when her mother and I returned to the waiting room, and my failure to be disturbed by her exposure of herself. I smiled.

Then visualizing Marsha's attack on Rene, I laughed.

Marsha looked at me in amazement. "I don't see what's funny," she said. Then she began to grin in response to me.

"I was thinking about poor Rene and the surprise she must have had," I said.

"Most people get mad when they are insulted. Most men I know would beat somebody up for calling them a queer. Doesn't anything make you angry?"

"Yes, Marsha, a lot of things make me angry, but this is just silly."

Marsha strode to the door holding her head high in mock indignation. "You know, you're a lousy psychologist," she said over her shoulder. She left the room, came back, stuck her head in the door and clowned through her parting remark, "Actually, you're a pretty good psychologist—for a queer."

Billy Joy was beginning to feel the full impact of her pregnancy and wished to talk about it.

"What am I going to do about this kid?" she asked me, indicating her abdomen.

"What do you want to do, Billy Joy?"

"Sometimes I think it's mine and I should keep it. Sometimes I wish it would go away. What can I do about it?"

I explained how a child could be placed for adoption.

"What if I decide to place it and then change my mind?"

"That's your privilege right up to the time they take the baby away."

"They can't make me give it up? After all, I'm a juvenile."

"Not about the baby. As a mother, you are an adult and no one can decide for you."

"You're kidding. Not the judge, nor my parents, nor anyone?" She was thoughtful. "Suppose my parents decide they want to keep the baby until I'm ready for it?"

"They can't have it without your permission. Only if you

abuse the baby can anyone take it away. They can do that to anyone, but they seldom do."

"So I can decide for myself," she said, pleased at the thought.

She left without making a decision, enjoying the privilege of having the decision to make, debating for a few days even whether she would talk about it with the social worker from Child Welfare.

The reception clerk came to my door with a letter in her hand. "Is Billy Joy Kepler your case?" she asked.

"Yes, she is," I said, wondering why the clerk seemed disturbed.

"I think you should read this. I censor the girl's mail, you know, and I'm supposed to call the counselor's attention to anything that doesn't look right. This is a letter from Billy Joy's brother and it's pretty radical."

"We censor the girl's mail?" I asked. I should have known about this before now but I didn't, and I reacted with shock.

"I'll leave it here with you," the clerk said. "Let me know whether to send it on to the girl."

I started to read:

Dear Kid sister,
I heard you were pregnant and in the reformatory and I wanted to let you know how I feel about it—

The indecent feeling of invading someone's privacy crept over me and I refused to read further. I resolved to question the need for censorship when the time was right, and returned the letter to the clerk, telling her that Billy Joy should have it.

Billy Joy stormed into my office the next morning. "My big brother has gone off his rocker!" she said.

I waited.

"I got a crazy letter from him. Some Commie must have got ahold of him. He's going to college over at State now and—he's crazy."

"Crazy how?"

"Like he's not going to let them draft him because Pa made him eat fresh pan fried prairie oysters on the range. And like he's going to turn the ranch over to the coyotes if he gets a chance, because Pa and Uncle Ambrose used to make him fetch hot coals in his hands to light their smokes. He says there ain't a thing wrong with Mexicans and niggers and Catholics and Jews and that we just hate them because we're mean.

"Jack's a great one to talk about being mean. He was meaner than I was. When a Mexican family moved in on a farm near us, he used to roll big rocks down the mountain on them to see if he could kill them. He used to operate on a live rabbit to see its innards work. Once he caught a muskrat in a trap and it was still alive and he put a stick up for it to bite and then measured how deep the teeth marks went. He was a tough guy. Now he sounds like a sissy. I hate sissies. I feel like smashing their heads like you smash a rotten melon."

"It really upsets you, Jack's wanting to stop hating," I said.

"What's wrong with hate? You're supposed to hate evil, and Commies and all your country's enemies and snakes and other varmints. All those things would take over if you didn't hate them, wouldn't they?" she asked.

I didn't think she wanted an answer so I waited.

"Well, wouldn't they?" she asked, still louder.

I still didn't think she was ready. "You think your brother is wrong."

"Of course he's wrong. He's damn wrong. What would he do if some Communist geeks came up to our house and tried to rape my mother and me? Let them do it?"

"You're scared, aren't you?"

"I'm not scared. If my brother's a damned sissy and wants to live with a bunch of pacifist fags, I'll defend myself. I've got a 38 and a 30-30 and 16 guage of my own and I'll use 'em when I need to." She stopped to breathe.

"That's one way you agree with your father," I said.

"Yeah. Jack said Pa was a silly superpatriot who loved the flag and hated his country. He said Pa's patriotism was just an excuse to kill foreigners. Where would this country be if every-body talked like that? We'd be overrun with Communists, that's what." She began to sound less sure. "What am I going to do about Jack? After all, he's my brother."

Now I felt she wanted an answer. "I don't know, Billy Joy. You don't seem to understand what is happening to him."

"I don't. What is happening to him?"

"Do you agree with your parents about all their ideas?"

"No. But I hate the same things they do."

"Part of growing up is deciding in what ways you don't agree. You form your own value standards. That's what we call our ideas about what's good and bad—a value standard. Col-lege is a place where all the value standards are studied and questioned. Jack is deciding right now that he doesn't agree with his father's value standard at all."

"He sounds freaky to me."

"It seems to you, Billy Joy, that there are a lot of danger-ous animals and people in the world and that if you don't kill them first, they'll kill you."

"Certainly. Of course."

"So the world is just naturally a violent place where you have to be ready to be violent."

"Yeah. And men have to do most of the killing to protect the women and babies. But Jack doesn't seem to think there is any danger from those things. He acts like our family is the ones that are dangerous."

"Right. That's what he thinks."

"Are you trying to give me the same line? Are you a Commie? I always heard that a lot of psychologists are Commies."

"I don't think it's my job to sell you any value standard. You have to decide what you believe. I think a person can decide better if he understands. And you asked me if I am a Communist. No, I'm an old fashioned Jeffersonian Democrat."

"I don't know what you are talking about. If a thing is right, it's right; and if it's wrong, it's wrong," she said.

I smiled. "What else do you want to talk about?" I asked.

"I don't know. This letter really bothers me, being from my own brother."

"I understand that, Billy Joy. It must be confusing."

"If I don't think the way I think, I don't know what I'll think."

"I think you are being courageous to think about it at all, Billy Joy."

"I feel like I have to. Jack and I used to hate each other when we were kids, except once in a while when we were way out on the range somewhere away from the house. I could hardly wait for him to leave home. Then when he ran away from home and worked on a ranch in Montana, I began to miss him. He'd come home once in a while and fight with Pa and talk a long time with me and then he'd go again. Now, he's the only one that says I'm a good kid and he doesn't care if I am in a reformatory or pregnant or anything and he says he wants to help me. Jesus. He wants to help me. Nobody else wants to help me. I ain't got nobody else but him."

She watered up in the eyes but stopped the tears as bravely as John Wayne, so I throttled my sympathy, too.

"Why don't we invite Jack up here to talk things over?" I suggested.

"Now there's a good idea, sir," she said. "I got a lot of

things to talk over like what I'm going to do about this kid I'm going to have."

"You invite him. Tell him to let you know when he's coming, and I'll arrange the time and place for you. O.K.?"

"O.K." she said. "But sir, I'm telling you, I ain't letting Jack change my mind about rattlesnakes. I really do hate rattlesnakes."

After weeks of our waiting, the correspondence tracing Saralee's father had finally located him. A succession of police departments knew of him for minor offenses. He was finally convicted of auto theft and manslaughter in Arizona, and was now serving a five-year term in the state prison. I braced myself to tell Saralee about him.

She came to the interview still intense but in better control of herself. "Hello, Doctor. I went home for two days, you know."

"I know. How was it?"

"Oh, just great, but I could hardly stand it to come back here."

"How do you feel now, Saralee?"

"Mostly O.K., because I think there is some hope of going home for good."

"We'll do our best. Miss Swanson was bothered before, because you wouldn't help yourself. It seemed as though you always ran away just in time to prevent her from doing anything to help."

"That was dumb, wasn't it?" said Saralee.

"Maybe. But maybe you did it for a reason."

"What reason?"

"I don't know," I said. "Can you think of any?"

"I was afraid sometimes that my mother didn't want me."

"Then if you had been sent home, you might have found out that she didn't want you."

"So I was scared to go home? she asked. "I *was* kinda scared to go home. But now I'm not."

"I wonder if the years you were away from your mother made you afraid she didn't want you," I said.

She puckered her lips and became tearful. "Sometimes I think nobody wants me."

I let her think for a moment. Suddenly she said, "Oh, I almost forgot. Will your wife and you be chaperones at our Junior-Senior Prom?"

"When is it, Saralee?"

"Next week Friday, April 29th, at eight thirty P.M."

"I think we can. I'll check with my wife and let you know tomorrow for sure. I'm flattered at the invitation."

"Oh, everyone voted for you," Saralee said.

"Where do they get the boys for the prom, Saralee?"

"From the air force base. They bring them over on a bus."

"It should be fun," I said.

We were silent for a moment. I hesitated, then said, "Saralee, I have some news. The letter is back about your father. We know where he is." I held up the letter.

She reached forward, grabbed it from my hand and devoured the contents, standing and reading with her lips. As she finished she gave a great sigh. "Is *that* all. He's in jail." She spread her hands dramatically. It was as though she had said he was in church.

"Why didn't he write me?" she asked.

"Maybe he felt ashamed."

"That's dumb. But maybe he was. Besides, he can't write very well. His spelling is highly creative, I always say. Can I write to him right now?"

"Perhaps you'd like to talk with him on the telephone."

"Honestly? Do you mean it?" She waved her hands with excitement.

"I can't promise we'll get through to him, but I'll try."

While I placed the call, Saralee paced, bit her fingernails, got up, then sat down and rocked herself on the back legs of the straight chair. When I reached the prison, I had to explain my call to the warden. He responded promptly, saying that, of course, a father should be allowed to talk on the telephone to his daughter.

Finally, I was speaking to Saralee's father. "Mr. Austin, did they tell you that this call is from your daughter? Good. Here's Saralee."

Mr. Austin did not sound like a gypsy. He sounded like a plaintive, middle-aged father.

I placed the receiver in Saralee's trembling hands and walked out the door so they could talk. As I pulled it shut, I heard her crying out across the years and the miles, bringing the gypsy home, "Oh, Daddy. Daddy? Daddy."

Billy Joy's brother, Jack, had come and gone and I had missed him, but Billy Joy wanted to talk about his visit.

"Jack's not crazy," she said. "He's just full of arguments like he always was, and like I said to him, he's deciding on his standard of values. He's got a point. He says Pa makes us hate him by being mean and then Pa teaches us to feel hate to other people instead of to him. I think Jack's right. He carries it too far, but I think he's got a point."

"I'm glad you were able to understand each other."

"Yeah, we could have talked for hours more. Like Jack says, Pa's wanting to desex me is more of his meanness, so he can have control over me. And that's right. Pa's nervous if he doesn't have perfect control over everybody."

"Jack really helped you figure things out, didn't he?"

"Yes, sir, he did. I even decided now what to do about the baby. Jack says that he and I are liable to do the same mean things to our kids Pa did to us. He says we have to learn to live without hating or else we'll hate our own kids. So I'm ready to talk to the social worker."

"I'll arrange it. You think you aren't ready to love this baby enough."

"As a matter of fact, I've been hating it before it was born. Now that I've decided to give it up, I've begun to want it. I'd better see the social worker right away. Besides I'm due to foal in three weeks."

She was carrying the baby low and looked so pregnant that she gave me a familiar feeling of inadequacy, knowing I was useless if delivery came.

XI

Bonnie and I arrived a few minutes early for the Junior Prom. The school gym had received the conventional treatment. The theme of the occasion was "Hawaiian Holiday." Marsha and Saralee hurried to meet us and to drape a crepe-paper lei on each of us. They met Bonnie with a feminine poise that amazed me. Marsha escorted us to a pair of chairs and Saralee asked if she could bring punch or coffee.

When we were seated and Saralee had gone for the punch, Marsha said to me, "I couldn't get Jeannine to come tonight. Miss Loomis found a formal that fit her and both of us talked to her but she just wouldn't come."

"It's all right, Marsha," I said. "She may feel better not to come this time."

Other girls were arriving. As they did, each looked at me with a yearning to be recognized, and at Bonnie with frank and friendly curiosity. Miss Swanson came to meet Bonnie, and the two of them renewed their old relationship. Presently the counselor said to Bonnie, "Do you know about Billy Joy?"

"That's the very pregnant country girl?" asked Bonnie.

"She was," said Miss Swanson, including me now. "She had her baby this afternoon."

"Is she all right?" I asked.

"She was quite wonderful. She didn't let out a cry all during her labor. Afterwards when the nurse asked if she wanted to see her big boy—" Miss Swanson stopped to bite her lip to stop it from trembling "—Billy Joy said, no, if she saw the brat she might never give him up. It wasn't until the nurse was gone that she put the pillow over her face and cried. She's all right."

We sat in silent empathy and I gratefully thought, "Billy Joy is more than all right now. She has learned to love."

The drummer for the three piece male band slammed out a preliminary rhythm and two guitarists tuned up. Miss Loomis approached and discussed with me her firm conviction that social affairs were necessary for the development of the girls, despite the opinions of some board members to the contrary.

Girls moved in bevies to and from the bathroom, becoming more nervous as they anticipated the arrival of the bus from the air force base. The orchestra played a selection. Everyone listened for a moment and then resumed conversation.

There was a clock at the dark end of the gymnasium which nevertheless could be seen with little effort. Presently it was five minutes to nine, and everyone was becoming anxious.

Miss Loomis assured us all that the major in charge of special services at the base would see that a busload of boys came, but she hurried off to the telephone anyhow. Miss Swanson hastened to organize dancing lessons in various steps, with the girls who knew the steps teaching those who didn't. Miss Loomis slipped back beside me after a long fifteen minutes, confessing that she couldn't locate the major, nor anyone who knew anything about the bus.

The trio took a break, and black, bleak depression settled upon the girls.

"This looks like a scene from *Catch-22*," I said to Bonnie.

She looked at me, shocked. "This is perfectly horrible for these girls. Don't be insensitive." I made no more attempt to be lighthearted, or objective, or whatever it was I was being.

Ten minutes of fervent silent prayers, strained conversation, and punch drinking produced no busload of boys.

Miss Loomis bustled off for a last desperate attempt to locate the bus. After a hasty conference with Miss Swanson, I climbed on the bandstand and shouted. "Boys or no boys, we are going to have fun. Let's start with a talent show. Register your act or your friend's act with Miss Swanson. While that's going on, let's sing. Here's a song—you just sing each line after me. Now remember these words: 'and flagged the train.' " I started to sing in a raucous tone, fearful that the girls would think I was corny and wouldn't respond.

Bill Grogan's goat
Was feeling fine,
Ate three red shirts
Right off the line.

The orchestra established a rock beat behind the singing. For the first time in memory I liked rock music because the girls began to follow me with feeling.

Bill took a stick,
Gave him a whack,
And tied him to
The railroad track.
The whistle blew,
The train drew nigh,
Bill Grogan's goat
Was doomed to die.
He gave three groans
Of awful pain,
Coughed up those shirts (altogether now)
AND FLAGGED THE TRAIN.

The girls laughed and clapped, delighted to see me in this unprofessional role. I called, "Any requests?"

The girls began to yell to the orchestra for numbers they could sing. Soon some girls sang alone and then were coaxed up to the stage. Two dancers from the physical education class performed interpretive dances. The orchestra contributed a novelty selection. An Indian girl, named Helen, was bashful but consented to sing her own composition. She was awkward but commanded attention the moment she got on the platform. I whispered to Bonnie, "Helen was abandoned by her mother at the age of three and has been kicked around ever since." Helen began to sing, without accompaniment, a kind of blues, faltering deliberately on some tones.

Oh Mother, I miss you so,
Oh Mother, you'll never know.

One guitarist started strumming a soft, meandering background music.

My mother, what can I do?
My mother, I pray for you.
Mother, why don't you come,
Mother, why don't you come . . .

The melody wandered uncertainly. Helen closed her eyes and stopped abruptly. The girls were stunned for a moment and then gave her an ovation. She had spoken for all of them.

Three girls were taken to their cottage to fetch a record player. They then played the record and appeared in improvised costumes while doing the song in pantomime and mouthing the words.

After the talent show, Bonnie, Miss Swanson, and I gathered everyone around the orchestra, where we exhausted our supply of campfire songs, especially the kind one could slap or stomp to.

Then we began to tell stories—ghost stories, funny stories, and riddles. The girls came up with tricks, tongue twisters, and played hand-clapping games, in doubletime.

At twelve forty-five A.M. someone began tearing down the decorations, and a glorious paper fight developed. Miss Loomis clapped her hands at one o'clock, and they hastened to sweep up.

Then they filed out in their formals, switching off most of the lights. They sang like a choir of mended angels, "Good night, ladies. Good night, ladies."

The magic of the evening was slightly spoiled, or possibly enhanced, by the fact that one of the girls seduced the orchestra into smuggling her out the gate with them. The others sang as they danced up the hill to the cottages, "Merrily we roll along, roll along . . ."

Bonnie was pensive on the way home. "How strange," she finally said. "How sad, too. They are just kids, aren't they?"

I had not seen Lola Kittredge since the night of the board meeting. There was little hope of repairing the damage to our relationship, so I was happy to avoid her, thinking that time and other preoccupations might diminish her hostility.

Miss Swanson came to my office one day, looking anxious. "This morning I had a supposedly casual visit from Lola Kittredge," she said. "She asked me a lot of questions as though she were merely interested in my work. Then she asked me if you were helpful to me, and a lot of similar questions. I know that's what she really came for. It was exactly like talking to a big, hungry Siamese cat." Miss Swanson bared her teeth in mock savagery.

I laughed. "I haven't played all the games Mrs. Kittredge wanted me to play, but I'm hoping her resentment will blow over."

"I just don't want you to underestimate her," she said.

"I don't think I do. The best and only technique I can think of now is to be casual."

"All right, I'll help you ignore it, but Lola Kittredge is a manipulator and she makes me nervous."

"By the way," I said changing the subject. "We need to make some plans about Saralee."

"Good. She's certainly doing great. Wasn't she cute at the prom?"

"I'm inclined to think she has made all the progress she can make here and may backslide if we keep her too long."

"I know. I wish we could send her home and see that she had proper counseling there," she said. "Let's see, her mother is getting aid to dependent children. The child welfare worker could do a lot."

"Possibly there's a school counselor for emotional support at school, too," I said.

"Shall I find out?"

"Fine. Let's get a plan worked up. I'll talk to Miss Loomis about it; also to the teachers here, and the chaplain. We'll have to overwhelm Mr. Tellamon and the judge with our unanimous opinion," I said. We plotted carefully our attack.

It was the next day, when I was entering the office of the school principal, that I encountered Lola Kittredge. She and the principal were talking earnestly when I entered, and they paused with just barely perceptible awkwardness when they saw me.

"Good morning, Doctor," Lola said. "You look busy, as usual."

"I practice looking that way."

"I musn't interfere with the work of two such busy people," she said, moving out.

She managed to make her sinuous body movement communicate hostility. It annoyed me that in every encounter Mrs. Kittredge seemed to dominate, to establish a situation I could not cope with.

I turned to the principal, who was properly interested but noncommittal about Saralee's parole. She indicated she did not feel it was her function to make recommendations for parole. She would, however, provide a favorable report on Saralee's school adjustment, as well as a steadily improving report card.

A bell rang to signal the end of a class period as I was walking down the hall. The girls swarmed into the hall and greeted me with their usual enthusiasm. I had reached the door when Marsha came running. "Guess what, Doctor, guess what? I'm going to be valedictorian. All I have to do is get Bs on my final exams and I'll still be ahead. I'm going to give the valedictory, and probably my parents will come to hear me. Won't that be something?"

"You had better give a good speech," I said. "I'm coming, too."

"Will you help me with it?"

"Of course, if the school doesn't mind. You'd better get to class."

"O.K., but I had to brag, didn't I?"

"Of course. Congratulations, Marsha. I think the school should be honored to have such a brilliant valedictorian."

"Well, you know who's to blame, don't you?" She waved and was gone, and I had my reward for the week. Maybe for the month.

I had been watching Jeannine closely. The antidepressant was obviously increasing her energy flow and her appetite for life. The security of the fence and the routine of life were bringing a modest sparkle to her eyes and a flush to her cheeks. In interviews, however, she had remained defensive and guarded about her life on the Indian reservation, reluctant to share all of her problems with me. It would have been easy to break through the defense, but dangerous, and I felt it better to wait until she was ready. Meanwhile, she developed a relationship with me through discussing her problems in the institution.

One day I found her waiting for me in my office, sitting on the edge of a chair, clutching a letter in her hands. She offered it to me with trembling fingers. "It's from my mother. My father will be in town tomorrow for a meeting and he may come to see me." Her breathing was shallow and her voice small.

"Did you want me to read this, Jeannine?"

She nodded and I read.

May 5

Dearest Daughter,

I think so much about you and wonder so much how I have failed you. I pray daily for understanding, but still do not understand. Your father spends more and more time with these underprivileged children of God, seeking, I am sure, to atone in hard work for the failure he does not understand.

We hope you are happy and with God in that place. Remember He is there as He is here. Wherever people need Him most He is most to be found. Perhaps it is His way to bring understanding first to you and through you to us.

Your father will be in town Thursday May 7th to talk with the mission board and may come out to see you in the afternoon if there is time. I yearn to come but my back is worse lately and I must rest every morning and every afternoon.

Be good, my daughter. Find God and come back to us.

Love, Mother

"Do you want to see your father if he comes, Jeannine?" I asked as I finished reading.

She trembled and shook her head.

"You don't have to see him if you don't want to," I said.

She sighed. "That's why I ran away."

"To avoid your father?"

"Yes."

"Not your mother?" I asked.

"Oh, no. Mother is sweet and good. I can't bear to hurt her." She paused and reached deeply into memory. "I don't want to ever see him. I can't ever see him again," she said. "I've got to tell you why, and I can't tell you." Her body contorted with the conflict.

"You want me to understand why."

"Yes, God knows why, but nobody else knows. Oh, help me."

Her agony told me that she must purge herself. "Just tell me, Jeannine. I'll help."

"He forced me to—to—." She looked at me with panic in her eyes and then looked away as the courage to tell me passed.

I couldn't let her be defeated and retreat again. "You have told me enough, Jeannine, so I know. In a way, I knew all along. Your father molested you."

She glanced up with a moment of alarm and seeing my compassion drew a great sigh. "Oh, how awful." She sobbed now, letting all the years of sorrow into spasms of grief. I wanted to touch her shoulder but knew I must not touch her at all.

Presently, between sobs, she said, "I hate him. He's an ugly man and I hate him."

"How old were you when it first happened?" I asked.

"It didn't happen all at once. When I was about eight years old, I knew something was wrong when he prayed with me." She shuddered. "When I was eleven, he hurt me and then I started to avoid him. I hate him. He's a filthy man and I hate him." She struggled to suppress the hatred. "It's wrong to hate," she said. "He always said it was my fault and I don't know why, but I felt like it was, even though I didn't do anything. Why do I keep feeling it was my fault?"

"Partly because he was your father, and he said it was your fault," I said.

"He said other things I didn't believe. I feel it was my fault."

"Perhaps you feel that because in some small way, you were human enough to enjoy it, Jeannine."

"No, I didn't," she said.

"Jeannine, there is a time when every little girl loves her father and wants to be very close to him. She is vulnerable. At that time it depends on the father."

"Do you have a daughter?"

"Yes, I have."

"Was she like that?"

"Yes, I think she was about six years old then, maybe even younger."

"I was still wrong."

"Perhaps, if you want to look at it that way. I just think it's a normal part of growing up. Your father was wrong, or ill."

"At least my mother was wonderful." She relaxed and cried more freely now. "I can't stop crying," she said. "It's wrong to hate."

"I don't know about that, Jeannine, but it's human. We all hate when we have been hurt badly."

"I could have forgiven him if he hadn't blamed me for it. He said I tempted him. I didn't. I didn't."

"He made you feel wicked and unclean and you hate him for it."

"I hate him for touching me, too. I guess I hate everything about him. I hate him for acting like it is wrong of me to like boys. Is it wrong?"

"Of course not," I said.

"Oh, I'm all mixed up," she said. "I just can't stop crying."

"Cry all you want, Jeannine." The tears continued and I handed her pieces of tissue until she began to subside. Finally I said, "I'll talk to your father tomorrow and you don't have to see him now—or ever."

"But I'll miss my mother."

"Someday you'll be mature enough and strong enough to see your father, and to make him behave just by looking at him," I said. "Look, you've used up all the tissue." I showed her the empty box.

She smiled a little.

"Jeannine, would you do me a favor? This office needs a picture on that wall. Would you paint one for me?"

"Yes, I'd like to try," she said, appraising the wall I had indicated.

The Reverend Mr. Post was extraordinary in appearance. His body was slight but his head was large and big domed. His blue eyes were magnified by thick lenses, gold rimmed. His chin was narrow and his mouth small, with shapely, rose-bud lips. His hands were huge, bony, and rough. The incongruity of these features made it difficult for me to integrate any impression of the personality.

The minister spoke slowly and carefully, in rehearsed fashion, as though from a pulpit. "Thank you, Doctor, for seeing me on such short notice. My wife and I feel the need of your guidance in planning our communications with Jeannine. We have, to be quite candid, wondered whether we should communicate at all. We seem to exacerbate the illness with our most well-intentioned contacts."

"As a matter of fact, Mr. Post, this girl is quite ill and at this point in the illness it is inadvisable for her to see you," I said.

"We will follow your advice to the letter, Doctor."

"Thank you," I said.

"My wife is a sensitive and devout woman who has been ill for many years. She reproaches herself continually for Jeannine's persistent efforts to run away from home and for the wild untruths that Jeannine invents to justify her actions. Anything you can do to reassure Mrs. Post that we are not to blame will save her much agony, I am sure. It might well prolong her life, which often seems to hang by a fragile thread.

"As to Jeannine, Doctor, from the day we took her from the orphanage, there was something strange about her. Her natural mother's mental health was questionable, and the instability of those early years surely left a mark. Then, of course, my mission isolated us for long periods of time from our own cultural groups. Jeannine, even as a young child, seemed unable to adjust to the life we must lead."

He continued to build a wall to protect himself from the child, but I kept my contempt for him under control because it seemed best for Jeannine.

Rene had sent word that she wanted to see me. I called the school and did not recognize the answering voice. "This is the psychologist. Will you send Rene Barbour over to my office, please?"

"Rene is talking to Mrs. Kittredge right now," the girl said. "I'll send her when she's through, Doctor."

While I waited, I walked to Miss Swanson's office and asked, "Do you know anything about board members interviewing the girls?"

"Oh yes," Miss Swanson said. "Lola Kittredge and her buddy, Mabel Anderson, have been very busy lately. They have talked with all the housemothers, a good many girls, and every probation officer that arrives."

"Thanks," I said. "I wish they'd leave the girls alone." I

said as I left abruptly and tried to reassure myself.

When Rene arrived she sat down and studied me.

"You wanted to talk to me, Rene," I said.

"You probably wanted to talk to me," she said.

"Not unless you want my help."

"You said I didn't trust men. You are half right. I don't trust women, either." She was belligerent.

"Maybe you haven't met anybody you can trust," I said.

"Boy. You aren't kidding."

"You don't know about me, yet," I said.

"I think I'll give you a fair chance."

"Thank you, Rene, and I'll try not to let you down."

"Do you know why I'm really in this hole?" she asked.

"Your commitment order says, 'truancy, curfew violation, and incorrigibility.' "

"That's all true, but the real reason is to keep me from talking."

"How do you know?" I asked.

"Because I haven't done anything lately, and right after I told my probation officer some things, I got sent here."

"That sounds logical," I said. "But I don't see what you could tell that would be so important."

"Well, listen. After my daddy left my mother, he didn't send her any money. I was only about ten years old then, so I don't know exactly what happened, but she went to some lawyer to see what she could do about it. She saw that lawyer quite a lot for about three years, and he'd take her out and bring her home late at night. His name is John Kraus and I thought they were going to get married, but they never did, and pretty soon they stopped going together. Now Mama goes away sometimes at night all dressed up, and a taxi brings her back.

"The funniest thing about it, though, is that once I looked in her purse and there was a check from John Kraus for $600.

And once I saw him downtown in a store and he was really nice to me and he asked how my mother was, like he hadn't seen her in a long time."

"What do you conclude from all this, Rene?"

"I think Mama is going with some man that's awfully rich or important, and he pays her money through John Kraus."

"And it upsets you?"

"It makes me puke. Then something else happened that really did it. When Mama went out, I began to have my friends come to the house. We didn't do anything so bad, but we smoked a little pot and drank some beer and played records. The neighbors complained and we got caught and that's when I first got a police record. Then it got worse and Mama sent me to talk to our priest. I told him everything, and he told me I should be good even if I didn't think my mother was doing right. I thought he was a good man and went to see him three or four times, and I really was studying hard in school and behaving myself. Then he wanted to see my mother, so she went to see him. Late that night she came home. She looked to see if I was alseep and I pretended I was, and I heard her with the priest on the couch. Ick." She covered her face with her hands for a moment.

"This is what you told your probation officer?"

"Yeah, I told him all of this. He said he didn't believe me, and they locked me up anyway."

"What did the judge say?"

"I never even saw a judge."

"That's quite a story."

"Do you believe me?"

"Yes, I believe you," I said.

When Rene was gone I made my notes. I debated about putting them in the regular case file, but knowing Lola Kittredge was prowling for information, I decided to lock them in my desk instead.

XII

Graduation day was on Saturday, the Memorial Day weekend, to make it possible for parents from all over the state to attend. The ceremony was to be at two thirty P.M., and the governor had consented to come and speak. I came into my office in the morning to talk with some parents I had been unable to see before. I hoped that Marsha's parents might be among them.

Late in the morning I saw board members and a few probation officers moving into the board room. Mr. Tellamon and Mrs. Garvey were there. I ran into Miss Loomis in the file room with her secretary and was alarmed over the superintendent's appearance. Her grey hair, usually under some control, was hanging loosely around her neck. Her hands were working with greater agitation than usual and her head was wobbling unsteadily. She was distracted, and the secretary was reminding her of the files she would need. I was embarrassed for her. I wanted to ask about her health, but she was trying to conceal her distress, so I left quickly to spare her.

At noon I went home for Bonnie. When we arrived at two P.M., the graduation crowd was already assembling. After seating Bonnie, I went back to a classroom to see the eleven graduating seniors, delivering to each of them a compact prettily wrapped by Bonnie, and a card of congratulations.

Marsha was standing at a window looking frightened and

dazed. She scarcely saw me, and barely mustered a "thank you" for the gift.

"My parents aren't here yet." She looked out the window again, and walked back and forth in front of it.

"Good luck on your valedictory," I said. She didn't answer.

As I went back to the auditorium I felt slightly hurt over her indifference to me. I chided myself; of course, her parents were infinitely more important to her. The seats were almost taken now. Miss Swanson was supervising the ushers, and I asked her to save seats for Marsha's parents.

I rejoined Bonnie. We were seated directly behind a group of younger girls. By ones and twos the girls turned around to wave, smile, or be recognized by me. Some knew Bonnie and waited for her to remember them.

"This is quite a family of daughters you have here," Bonnie said.

"Well, they're more sugar than spice today," I said.

Jeannine stepped up to the piano. She was in a white dress. Her hair was pulled back from her face and tied in a white bow at the nape of her neck, Victorian fashion. It accentuated her small, heart-shaped face and large velvet eyes.

"What a beautiful child," Bonnie said.

"That's Jeannine Post," I told her.

With a vigor I did not know she possessed, Jeannine struck the full chords of "Pomp and Circumstance." I glanced around at Miss Swanson, who pointed to two empty seats.

The massive doors in back were swung wide now, and the seniors came through in cap and gown, two by two, in rhythm to Jeannine's perfect beat. The crowd stood in their honor. Marsha walked last, alone. She looked desperately at Miss Swanson as she entered, and Miss Swanson glanced in response at the two empty seats. Marsha's face froze, her eyes transfixed and unseeing.

Following the graduates was the governor beside Miss Loomis. She was neat again but her face was ashen. I could detect a certain movement of her head. I wondered about Parkinson's disease, but then reproved myself for a sidewalk diagnosis. Mrs. Purdy and Bishop Elder completed the procession, and all stood finally at their places on the platform. Bishop Elder invoked divine blessing on the gathering, and sat down.

Miss Loomis welcomed the audience in a halting voice. The governor orated with pride befitting his ambition to be a senator. Claudia sang "The Battle Hymn of the Republic" with lyrics rewritten to suit her own philosophy. The salutatorian said the country needed men and women of character and she felt the senior class would make great contributions.

One of the girls read the St. James version of *The Prodigal Son,* and then it was Marsha's turn to speak. I glanced back once more at the two empty seats. The back doors were closed and Marsha looked through them, seeing nothing else. Her voice was rehearsed and oratorical but plaintive.

"Parents, teachers, board members, Mr. Governor, classmates, housemothers, counselors and friends:

"This is an occasion for happiness. It is good to rest at the end of a task and celebrate its completion. It is good to gather together and congratulate each other on our mutual achievement. It is good to know that we as graduating seniors have in some measure lived up to the expectations of all of you.

"This is an occasion for sorrow, too. It is a little sad to know that we are leaving behind some of our childhood. It is sad to leave behind the friends, the teachers, the people who have been a part of our lives. It is sad that time goes on and we cannot have these years again.

"This is an occasion for thinking. It is time to think . . ."

Marsha faltered just a moment while one of the double doors opened slightly, but it was the janitor. She continued.

"It is a time to think how we shall live our lives. It is a time to consider what is important and what is trivial. It is a time to think how we can avoid old mistakes.

"This is an occasion for ending. It is the time for leaving behind childish things. It is the conclusion of high school, the last formal education for most of us. It is the end of a pattern of life we have known.

"This is an occasion for beginning. It is the commencement of adulthood. It is, we hope, the beginning of giving back to society what society has given to us. We will in some ways be born again, not necessarily better than before but better able to live than before.

"Yes, this is an occasion for happiness, an occasion for sorrow, and occasion for thinking, an occasion for ending, and an occasion for beginning.

"Every graduation everywhere is an occasion for these things. But for us here and now, graduating from high school in this institution is going back to life, rejoining the society we renounced, earning again the love of those we hurt, being accepted at home. Thank you, everyone, for that chance."

Marsha moved trancelike back to her seat and stared at the floor.

Miss Loomis called out the names and Mrs. Purdy handed out the diplomas. The bishop gave the benediction and the crowd was dismissed.

Bonnie and I watched for Marsha. She did not come forward off the platform and down through the crowd like the others, but disappeared backstage. We moved to find her as fast as we could, but everyone in our path required a greeting. At last we parted the curtains at the rear of the stage and entered a hall, where we heard her muffled sobs.

We found her hiding in a broom closet, curled up on the

floor, alone with her grief. Bonnie sat beside her to take her in her arms.

It took a long time for Marsha to sob herself out, to wash up, and to regain her poise. Then she agreed with me that something must have happened to prevent her parents arrival, and that a long distance telephone call might help. Bonnie and I put Marsha between us and drove up to the administration building. It was well after five o'clock by then, and we were surprised to see a number of impressive cars parked in front, including several with the state insignia.

"The board must be meeting again," I said.

"What do you mean—again?" asked Bonnie.

"Oh, they had an informal meeting this morning."

When we entered the building, an efficient-looking woman was impatiently pacing in the foyer.

"May I help you?" I asked.

"I'm Alicia Galloway of the *Times,* and you can tell me what this board meeting is all about."

"I'm afraid I don't know, and it wouldn't be my place to tell you if I did," I said.

"They refused me admittance on the grounds that it wasn't an official meeting, but rather a private conference with the governor. Something is cooking and this is not the proper way for the board of a public institution to treat the press," she said.

I grinned. "Sorry, I can't help."

Bonnie and Marsha had gone into my office. I joined them and placed the call for Marsha's parents. When the call came through, I handed the receiver to Marsha and took Bonnie into the hall with me.

Alicia Galloway was still there and I introduced her to Bonnie.

"They say reporters have a nose for news, but you must have a better reason than that for being here," I said.

"I have. The governor does not spend all of one day in an institution on a social visit, nor does he meet in secret session with the board of that institution for no reason. Who is Father Carney?"

"The Catholic chaplain. Is he there, too?"

"Yes. I'm probably wasting my time and won't even get an evasive statement from the governor. Could you give me an off-the-record tip?"

"I honestly don't know of anything unusual or news-worthy that is happening, even though I agree that something probably is happening."

Bonnie spoke up cheerfully. "Of course, that's what he says every night when he comes home. You know how uncommunicative men are."

"I know," Mrs. Galloway said. "Nothing has happened in my husband's office in fifteen years."

Marsha came bouncing out, her phone call completed. "The car broke down on the road. They had to go back home on the bus. That's why they couldn't make it. They'll be here to take me home next weekend."

While Marsha enthusiastically gave further details to Bonnie, I went back to my office. I automatically performed my usual ceremony, checking to see that windows were closed, desk cleared of confidential materials and the drawers locked. To my dismay I found the right top drawer open. Still acting automatically, I found the key on my ring and tried to turn the lock. It was jammed. I examined the lock and saw that it had been forced. Quickly I pulled the drawer and looked through several folders. Rene Barbour's folder was gone. I looked again. Jeannine's was gone, too. They were certainly missing, but nothing else had been taken.

On Monday morning when I entered my office I saw on my desk an oil painting on canvas and a note. The note read:

*Here is your painting. The oils will be wet for quite awhile,
but you can hang it if you are careful. I hope you like it and
I know Roy won't mind that I used his theme. I named the picture*
Promise.

Jeannine

The painting, done in delicate Indian style, showed a cot-
tonwood oasis, shading a quiet grassy bank in the foreground.
Behind the oasis a meadow sloped up to the mountain. Far
back, in delicate detail but evident on the open meadow, was
a deer leaping high and carrying a crown of antlers.

I removed an indifferent photograph from the wall, carefully hung my picture, and began some letters and reports.

Miss Swanson appeared at the door and looked back in
mock fear before entering.

"I shouldn't be seen talking to you," she said.

"Why not?"

"You mean you don't know? At this moment, Miss Loomis
is in the Methodist Hospital for an extensive diagnostic
checkup. Her office is occupied by a triumvirate which is operating the institution until further notice—Mrs. Purdy,
Mrs. Kittredge, and Bishop Elder. Mabel Anderson didn't
want to be left out, so she is acting as their executive secretary."

"Good God," I said. "Is it really that bad?"

A secretary knocked on the door. She handed each of us
a mimeographed notice. It stated:

To: All staff members
From: Mr. Lex Woolman, Chairman, Board of Governors
Subject: Administrative emergency
  *I regret to inform you that Miss Loomis is seriously ill and at
  present on leave from her post as superintendent. We confidently
  expect her return in good health at a later date. Meanwhile three
  board members have consented to temporarily maintain the con-*

*tinuity of Miss Loomis's leadership by administering the institu-
tion as an executive committee of the board. We hope all of you
will continue efficiently with your duties as before.*

Signed, Lex Woolman

Miss Swanson said, "Lex Woolman didn't write that. It's
literate."

"It's also legal, I suppose," I said.

Miss Swanson got up to leave. "I wonder where they will
put the guillotine."

"In the foyer, with the Inquisition's bird cage beside it,
I suppose."

"Is there any hope?" she asked.

"If there is, it is in Bishop Elder, I think."

With Miss Loomis gone I found myself emotionally disor-
ganized. When the summons came to report to the superintendent's office, I could only remind myself to be cautious.

Mrs. Purdy was in a Queen Victoria pose at the superintendent's desk. She was flanked by Mrs. Kittredge and Mabel
Anderson, one on each side of the desk. Bishop Elder was not
there. Everyone spoke formally and I responded politely.

Mrs. Purdy began the discussion. "Doctor, we are reviewing parole actions and summer plans for some of the girls.
Several you work with are involved."

"I'll be happy to review the plans with you," I said.

"Let's see, who are these girls?" She fumbled with some
papers.

Lola Kittredge reached over, pulled out the appropriate
paper and pointed to the name.

"Oh, yes," Mrs. Purdy said. "First, Marsha Mabry. I
remember her. The capable girl who gave the speech at
graduation. You have arranged for her parole?"

"Yes. The board, the judge, everyone has approved," I
said. "She will return home to her parents. There's a lot of

friction in the home but we think Marsha is mature enough
to live with it now."

Lola Kittredge spoke slowly and decisively. "I think the
record clearly indicates the doctor is right."

"Yes, I suppose so," Mrs. Purdy said. "However, the governor feels we should review these paroles with great care."

"Saralee Austin is the next one," said Mabel Anderson.

Lola Kittredge picked up the folder and said, "I'm no
expert in these matters, Doctor, but I can't help wondering
why you recommended parole when this girl has run away so
many times and is going back to a very questionable home."

All three women looked at me inquiringly.

"I believe that this was carefully explained in my letters
to the judge," I said. "Admitting that Saralee's home leaves
much to be desired, we should bear in mind that it is her home.
No other would be acceptable to her. She has deep attach-
ments to her mother and to her brothers and sisters. When
she is away, she suffers from homesickness. I mean she is ill,
seriously ill, and in pain. She is not very treatable here for that
reason. We have arranged for her to have systematic treatment
from a social worker while she is at home, and we believe she
will improve there."

"Of course, as you know, Doctor, the legislature created
this Home not as a clinic, but as a house of correction." Lola
Kittredge was enjoying her role as inquisitor. "Did you know
also that Mr. Tellamon is bitterly opposed to this action and
feels that the series of letters and testimonials to the judge is
going over his head?"

"Yes, I am aware of Mr. Tellamon's opposition."

"I gather you question his judgment."

"Mrs. Kittredge, you need to know that none of the girls
from that district are ever encouraged to return home. Not
only do Miss Loomis, Miss Swanson, and I feel that Saralee
must go home, but we also believe we are executing the policy

of the board to take the most effective action for each girl."

Mrs. Kittredge would not be sidetracked. "But you *are* questioning Mr. Tellamon's judgment."

"I suppose so. You could equally say he is questioning our judgment. There are bound to be some disagreements. I hope the board will back this request because I think the judge will listen favorably."

"Doctor, tell me honestly—what do you think of Mr. Tellamon?"

I thought carefully and delayed so long in answering that Mrs. Purdy began to tap her fingers on the table and then saved me from answering. "Well, this committee is not conducting a hearing on the qualifications of the probation officer. The only point on which I find myself in sympathy with your position is that this girl's mother is even more immoral than the girl. Yet the girl is confined here and the mother is free. That does not seem just. Again, however, we are not here to judge whether the mother deserves to be free in society, but whether the girl does. What do you wish to say about that?"

"Mrs. Purdy, I am unable to think in terms of what Saralee deserves. It seems better to me to think in terms of what is best for Saralee and society."

"Precisely, Doctor. That is saying the same thing in a different way. We will take Saralee Austin's parole under consideration to decide what is best for the child and for society." Mrs. Purdy spoke slowly and deliberately, leaving no doubt that the subject was closed.

Mrs. Kittredge picked up another folder. "Billy Joy Kepler. She had her baby and it was placed for adoption. Her parents and her probation officer want her released so they can secure medical treatment. Doctor, you are opposing the release. Would you explain why?"

"Billy Joy does not want to go home," I said. "She prefers to stay here."

Lola raised her eyebrows. "For heaven's sake why?"

"She feels safe here. Her parents are religious fanatics who propose to take her to quack doctors and have her desexed. The probation officer is encouraging the procedure. Billy Joy is understandably terrified."

"Judging from her history, a little desexing seems a good idea," said Lola. Mabel Anderson laughed loudly.

"But seriously, Doctor," Lola said. "You accuse the parents, the probation officer, the judge, and a religious group of bad judgment, all in the same breath. Her parents and the community want this girl back and I think we should send her back."

I leaned forward and tried to surmount the hostility. "Ladies, I believe you employed me here to use my professional skills and judgment in caring for these girls. I have done that. I protest that to send Billy Joy home under these conditions would be a violation of our responsibility to her."

Mrs. Purdy intervened. "We understand your position, Doctor, and will review the case carefully, I assure you. We still must consult with Bishop Elder."

"One other question, Doctor," said Lola, coy now. "I would so much appreciate your judgment about this. You work with Jeannine Post, I believe."

"Yes, I do."

"She seems such a sweet child and I believe she came from one of the better homes. If someone needed a sitter for their children, would Jeannine be reliable?"

"Yes, she would be reliable," I spoke slowly, "but she is a very sick girl and it's far too soon for her to leave the security she feels here. Later, perhaps, she will need a chance like that. Not now."

"Thank you, Doctor," said Lola.

"Yes, thank you very much," said Mrs. Purdy, rising abruptly to conclude the interview.

Thinking about it later, I wondered why I had not re-signed at this point, either quietly or with public protest. Some commitment to my patients and to myself compelled me to continue. Furthermore, things were happening so fast that I could not digest them and I found it hard to make abrupt decisions.

By the second day of committee rule, all the staff knew that I was under fire and I was acutely aware that most of them were avoiding me. Miss Swanson and one or two others made a point of declaring their loyalty to me. The other staff members stayed away, but the faith of the girls in me was almost absolute.

It was Rene's day for an appointment, and when she failed to come I called her housemother.

"Rene is in lock, Doctor," I was told.

"What happened?" I asked.

"She was impertinent to the board members, I am told."

"I see. Thank you."

I went down to the basement cells, unlocked Rene, and brought her back with me to my office.

She looked reprovingly at me.

"You are angry with me, Rene," I said.

"You told everything I said to those women—those board women."

"No, I didn't. I jotted down some notes about what you said and I locked them in my desk. Someone broke into the desk and took them," I said.

"I can't trust anybody."

"I can understand your feeling that way, Rene, but it isn't true. Right now you can trust me. At least, you can trust me to do my best."

"O.K. But they knew what I said about the priest and they asked me a whole lot of questions."

"Did the questions upset you?" I asked.

"No, but it's hard to figure out. They acted kind of *afraid* of me. They locked me up but they keep coming back and being nice to me. Tell me, what's going on, Doc?"

I thought about it. "I don't know, Rene. I really don't. But I'm going to give you one very strange piece of advice. It won't be good for you to let people know that you like or trust me. Pretend you can take me or leave me. Do you understand? I don't even want you to be seen talking to me if we can avoid it. I suspect that some board member is afraid I'm going to cause trouble for the people you talked about. If they don't see us together they won't be so afraid of you. So go on now, and have somebody else put you back in lock."

"O.K. I'm going. I think I get the idea. Doc, I never met anybody like you before. You keep acting like kids were people with feelings and rights like anybody else. You'll probably get yourself in a lot of trouble that way. So, if you ever need my help, just ask for it."

XIII

Jeannine didn't come to group therapy, and I asked the others about her.

"She went out on a baby sitting job this week," said Frances.

"For Mrs. Kittredge, I think," said Marsha. "She was nervous about going out. I don't think she's ready. Do you?"

I didn't answer and I hoped my alarm didn't show. Mrs. Kittredge had ignored my emphatic opinion. She had declared war and now I could expect anything.

"Isn't Miss Loomis coming back?" asked Billy Joy. "The board is screwing everything up around here."

"It will depend on her health, I am sure," I said.

"Could some of us go see her?" asked Marsha. "I wonder sometimes if she knows I'm really sorry for calling her names. She's a great old lady."

"I'm sure she knows how you feel, Marsha. I think it's too soon to visit her, but why don't you write her a card or a letter?"

"Let's do it right now," said Billy Joy.

I fetched some writing materials and they all settled down to write. As they finished and handed the letters to me for mailing, Frances asked, "Did you know that I'm going to have a trial visit with my mother all next week?"

"And I'm being discharged next Sunday," said Marsha. "I'm glad, but I'm scared."

Saralee was puzzled by that. "What are you scared of?" she asked.

"I don't know exactly," answered Marsha.

"I'm not really scared, but I'm nervous," said Frances.

"I don't even want to go," said Billy Joy. She still seemed depleted from the experience of having her baby. "The board is considering my case and I'm afraid they're going to make me go home."

I explained to all of them that confinement in any institution grew to be a curious security from the world and that leaving that security usually produced anxiety.

"I don't get it," said Saralee in response to my remarks. "I want to go home and I'm scared not to go. I want to go home and they aren't going to let me. Mrs. Purdy told me so."

"I was afraid of that," I said.

"They said I hadn't earned it yet and that I'd be glad later they didn't let me go. But I have to go. I can't stand it anymore." She beat her hands on her head and her eyes were desperate.

"Take it easy, Saralee," said Marsha.

"I won't take it easy. Can I tell you a secret?"

"Sure. Of course. You can trust us," the others agreed.

"No, I mean do you really promise not to tell on me? You too, Doctor?"

"He has to keep secrets. It's his professional responsibility," said Marsha.

"Is that true?" Saralee asked me.

"I do have to keep most things confidential. There are some exceptions. For example, if you were in serious danger, I would have to try to keep you from hurting yourself."

"Oh, I'll be safe. Do you promise?"

"Perhaps you shouldn't tell me your secret."

"I want to tell you because I don't want you to be mad at me about it. Can I tell you?"

"It's up to you. You'll have to trust me to use my judgment."

"O.K.," Saralee said, "I think I'm going to trust you because you tried to help me and get me out. You didn't do it, but you tried." She paused and then burst out with her secret. "I'm going to run away and go home. They'll catch me and bring me back but I'll be home long enough to make life worth living."

"Do you think it's worth it?" asked Marsha. "They'll put you in lock."

"I've been in lock before and I can stand that. It will be worth anything to be home for just two days. Besides, Mama will hide me, so I can probably be there for a week."

"You tried to run before and goofed it," Frances said.

"I didn't plan it before. This time, I'm being smart."

"You'd better check it over with us," said Billy Joy. "What's your plan?"

"Well, tomorrow afternoon the nurse takes me downtown to the dentist, and there are usually about eight girls, so the nurse can't stay with all of us. I'll be one of the first ones in line, so the nurse won't think I'm trying to get away. Then I'll have a flapping shoe strap and I'll stop to fix it right at the corner. When she looks back, I'll be gone. I can outrun her anyway. As soon as I'm safe, I'll call my cousin. He works here for a construction company and he usually drives home on the weekend. He'll take me home."

"That's a good plan," Billy Joy said.

"How long have you been shut up, Saralee?" Marsha asked.

"Nineteen months and eleven days, and I had one two day trial visit and that's all. My mother hasn't got a car and she was here only two Sundays in the whole time."

"I guess I don't blame you. I hope you make it home," Marsha said.

"Good luck," Frances said.

"Thanks, I'll make it this time."

Billy Joy had been thinking. "Hey, I think I'll get a toothache and come with you. I won't stick around with you very long because I want to get caught and you don't."

"You want to get caught?" asked Saralee.

"Yeah, I'll go shoplifting. That's the best way to get caught. See, if I have another offense before I get discharged, I won't get sent home."

"Hey, that's intelligent," said Frances.

Marsha added, "And if they really plan to desex you, I don't blame you for wanting to stay here. But you can't stay here forever, Billy Joy."

"I'll be eighteen years old in five months and I can ship out from home legally then. The trick is to shoplift exactly five month's worth. Any suggestions?"

We all laughed.

"I hope I don't ever have to explain this group therapy session to anyone," I said. "First one girl plans to run away and now another one is joining her. That's progress."

"Why don't we all escape and have a party?" asked Frances.

Marsha was serious. "Every person has to do the best thing for her. I don't see what else Saralee and Billy Joy can do. If you have a big problem, and you don't do something dramatic to let people know about it, they don't pay any attention to the problem. On the other hand, if you protest and make a good show of it, something gets done."

"That's right," Billy Joy said, "but sometimes they don't do what you want them to. They do something else you don't want."

"Protesting gets a reaction, but not necessarily exactly the reaction you want," I said.

"It doesn't matter what I do, I don't get the reaction I

want," said Saralee. She turned to me. "Are you against me going? Are you going to stop me?"

"We're putting you on the spot, aren't we?" Marsha said to me.

"Yes, a little bit," I said. "The board members know that we have this group therapy session and they could decide that it didn't do any good."

"So you're going to turn me in?" Saralee began to cry.

"No, I'm not. I just have to be honest about my feelings, too. And you have to know the effects of what you are going to do."

"If the board says it's a failure when it isn't, and stops group therapy, that's their fault, not ours," Marsha said.

"What they do is their responsibility. What you do is your responsibility," I said.

"Yeah, I guess so," she said.

The others were watching this clash intently, not being accustomed to seeing me assert myself.

"I don't know what to do. I don't know what's right," Billy Joy said.

Saralee was whimpering so, Billy Joy turned on her. "Oh, shut up and think."

Saralee shut up.

"It isn't easy to decide what's right, is it?" I said.

Frances said, "There's some right and some wrong both ways."

"It seems to me," said Marsha, "that the harm in going is only a possibility and that the harm to Saralee and Billy Joy in staying here is a bad and sure thing. I think they should go if they decide to. I won't blame them. It's up to them."

"Me too, that's what I think," said Frances. "It's up to them."

All of them looked at me. "Yes," I said, "It's up to each of them."

As the group left the board room, Mrs. Winifred came by. She had not quite forgiven me yet for finding her less than perfect in her gushing over Jeannine. She embraced the girls now and glanced at me with a subtle victory in her eyes. I ignored it and went to my office.

It was a few minutes later when I walked back down the hall and found Saralee and Frances still standing, one on each side of Mrs. Winifred, with her arms about their waists.

"The girls tell me they are having a lovely time in your group sessions," Mrs. Winifred said, releasing them. We watched the girls dash away, hand in hand.

"My, Doctor, aren't they the young ladies now?" she said.

"Yes, I think we can be proud," I said.

"Saralee talks and talks about you. I'm sure she feels you should be sainted," said the housemother.

"Well, don't let her know the awful truth about me, will you?" I said as I left.

XIV

The following was not a Chamber of Commerce day. The wind began during the night, most of it 10,000 feet up carrying tons of dust from some desert west of us. By noon the ground wind blew in gusts that elevated local real estate, and the sun was visible only as a pale blur. For lunch I ate two bags of peanuts from the vending machine in the hall rather than dash fifty dusty yards to one of the cottage dining rooms.

I sat in my office and worried. Saralee and Billy Joy would be going downtown soon with the nurse and anything could happen to them when they broke away. Jeannine, I had learned, was employed every day by Mrs. Kittredge. With school not in session, her employment could last all summer. My appointments with Jeannine might be difficult to arrange. There was no diagnosis available yet for Miss Loomis. She had been sedated and sleeping last night when I visited her in the hospital. Rene was still in lock, and obviously the board was investigating and administering its way into a struggle with me.

An hour later, I was conferring with a child welfare worker by telephone when my office door was abruptly thrown open. Lola Kittredge and Mabel Anderson came in, dragging Jeannine Post by the arms. They pushed her into a chair and stood facing me.

"Emergency here, I'll call you back," I said, and hung up the phone. I faced the angry women.

"I thought you said, Doctor, that this girl was reliable," Lola Kittredge said.

"I did, and she is, but she was taken from this institution against my advice." I tried to get Jeannine to look at me, but her face was white beneath a coating of dust, and she stared at the floor.

"She left my child and ran away. Fortunately, a neighbor came over by accident and discovered my boy was alone."

"Yes, we met this *thing* running down the highway when we were on the way home." Mabel pointed at the girl.

"Young lady, do you realize that if something had happened to my child, you would be responsible?" Jeannine didn't move so Lola seized her arm and shook it. "Answer me! Do you hear? Answer me!" There was no response. Lola turned to me. "Well, Doctor, would you like to demonstrate *your* method?"

"Would you ladies sit down?" I said. I waited until they did and then turned to Jeannine.

"Jeannine, can you talk a little bit? If you left that child alone you do owe Mrs. Kittredge an explanation."

Jeannine made little notions with her lips and looked hopelessly at me.

"Did you leave him?" I asked.

She nodded her head. Then she said, "No."

"I don't understand, Jeannine," I said.

"Mr. Kittredge was there." She spoke almost inaudibly, but Lola heard her.

"Well, that's fancy lying," said Lola.

"Mrs. Kittredge, would you like to hear her story?" I asked. "Jeannine, why did you run away from there?"

She placed her hands over her mouth and shook her head, refusing to speak.

I had to get her away from the women. I said to them, "I think I had better talk to Jeannine alone."

"My God, what a sap you are!" Lola shouted.

Jeannine looked up at Lola with a flash of hatred. She turned and whispered hoarsely to me. "He tried to do—like my father—"

I stood up. "I want to see my patient alone."

"And I want that girl in lock in fifteen minutes. Then I want to see you in the superintendent's office," Lola said, and stalked out with Mabel behind her.

Jeannine and I were silent. "I cause so much trouble," she finally said.

"No, Jeannine," I said. "I told them you weren't ready to take a job. They should have accepted my judgment."

"My father was right. Something is wrong with me."

"Are you hurt?"

"No, I ran away before anything happened, but something must be awfully wrong with me."

"Stop talking as though you were to blame for everything. There is a curious kind of conceit a person has when he thinks he's to blame for everything."

"Don't try to talk me out of it. I'm wicked and I don't deserve to live. Now I've got you in trouble, and I can't take any more."

I studied her a moment. "It's true, Jeannine, that I may not be working here much longer, but you had very little to do with it. I think you need help from a psychiatrist, and I am afraid I may not be in a position to help you any more. Would you mind going to the State Hospital?"

"I don't care."

"Please do care. I want you to get well."

"I'll do what you want me to," she said.

"I need to think carefully what is best for you. I have to take you down to the locked rooms for now, but I'll see you very soon."

As I took Jeannine into the isolation area, I could hear

Rene singing bawdily, "Thirty-four barrels of beer, thirty-four barrels of beer . . ."

"How are you, Rene?" I called.

"Oh, fine, doc. How are you?" she asked.

"I'll come down to talk with you later today."

I put Jeannine directly across the hall from Rene, thinking she might be a cheerful companion even through locked doors. At least it kept the girls in touch with each other.

As I closed the door on Jeannine, I felt again as though I were in another century. She was dressed in a simple, straight garment of some rough material, tied at the waist with a braided cotton belt. Her hair fell long around her face, and her feet were in sandals. My jaw tightened when the key turned.

The board members were convened in the superintendent's office. I was relieved to see Bishop Elder behind the desk. As I entered the room, Lola Kittredge made a sound back in her throat and hurried out of the room. I followed her with my eyes, uncomfortable to trust her out of my sight. Would she go to the basement?

"Hello, Doctor," said the Bishop. "Mrs. Kittredge is upset because your case notes impugn the integrity of certain clergymen and implicate the Lieutenant Governor."

"My case notes on what cases, Bishop Elder?" I asked.

The Bishop indicated two manila folders on the desk before him. "Rene Barbour and Jeannine Post," he read.

"Bishop Elder, if you have case notes indicating improper behavior of clergymen in connection with these girls, they have been stolen from my locked desk. They are confidential materials for professional use only, and were stolen."

"Doctor, it pains me that there seem to be some very serious conflicts among us. It is my earnest hope that we can all be cautious, charitable, and patient with each other. I think that the difficulty may be defined as mutual distrust, and probably arises out of misunderstanding. It is my intention to encourage the detailed review of each of these situations in an effort to restore confidence. I want you to know, Doctor, that my own confidence in you has not been shaken."

"Bishop Elder, my only hope is that your judgment will prevail. I am desperately concerned about what is going to happen to some of my patients. May I ask this committee's approval right now on an emergency action for one of the girls?"

"Of course, Doctor."

"Jeannine Post is seriously depressed. Several times Dr. Norden and I debated the advisability of sending her to the State Hospital for treatment. The conflicts that have arisen here recently over her case make treatment difficult. I would feel better about transferring her now. I am sure Dr. Norden will concur."

"It distresses me to hear that Jeannine is unimproved. The transfer seems proper to me. How do you feel about it, Mrs. Purdy?" the bishop asked.

"I see no objection, if the judge will agree."

"I will call the judge directly after this meeting to ask for his concurrence," the bishop continued. "If he agrees, we will send one of the social workers with her this afternoon. Is that satisfactory, Doctor?"

"Yes, Bishop Elder. Thank you. That will be a great relief."

The telephone rang. Bishop Elder picked it up. "Bishop Elder speaking. Yes, nurse. Yes, I remember Saralee. I don't understand."

Mrs. Kittredge came back and sat down. She listened intently as the bishop continued.

"What was Saralee's last name again? And the other one? Is there some procedure about runaways? Well, go right ahead and notify everyone as usual. Thank you." He hung up. "A girl named Saralee Austin and another named Billy Joy Kepler escaped from the nurse on the way to the dentist's office," he said.

Lola Kittredge smiled. "Bishop Elder, with your kind permission, I came upon some information this morning, and I didn't know what to make of it. I'm just not used to this kind of intrigue, but I think if I may call Mrs. Winifred, the housemother from reception unit, she might be able to shed some light on this escape."

"If you wish, Mrs. Kittredge," Bishop Elder said.

"I'll just go get her," said Lola.

Everyone sat awkwardly, waiting. I wondered if the end were in sight and tried to think what might be saved for each of the girls. My own situation was probably beyond repair.

Lola was back with Mrs. Winifred. "Now, you go ahead, Mrs. Winifred, just tell all of us what you told me this morning," said Lola.

"Yesterday," Mrs. Winifred said, "I was carrying on a conversation with Saralee and she was telling me how much she liked and trusted the doctor. She said she could tell him anything at all and trust him with it. She said she thought a girl could probably even tell him if she were going to run away, and not have him report her."

"Anything else, Mrs. Winifred?" asked Lola.

"No, that's all," the housemother said.

"You may be excused, Mrs. Winifred," said the bishop. She left reluctantly.

Lola narrowed her eyes as she turned on me. "Well, Doctor, did you know the girls were going to run away?"

"Yes, I did." I said.

"Did you inform anyone, or take steps to prevent it?"

"No, I didn't."

"Where are they now?"

"I don't know, Mrs. Kittredge, but I do know where they are going."

"Where are they going, Doctor?"

"I cannot and will not tell you, Mrs. Kittredge."

"Can I possibly understand you? You are refusing to tell the board of this institution where delinquent girls are hiding from the law?"

"That is correct, Mrs. Kittridge. It is privileged information."

"Can he do that?" Lola asked the bishop.

"Under some circumstances the doctor would be right, just as a minister of the gospel must respect similar information. Under these circumstances, I really don't know," said the bishop.

"Well, legal or not," Mrs. Kittredge said, "you certainly agree, Bishop Elder, that this is insubordination."

The bishop pushed his hands hard against the table top. "Must we press the issue?" he asked Mrs. Kittredge.

"Are we in charge, or is this man?" She stood up.

He turned to me, his voice wavering, "Doctor, if you could yield a point or two, there might be hope of resolution here."

I stood. "Bishop Elder, I regret to say that I think Mrs. Kittredge has asked a question that must be answered. I won't yield, because *I* want to know. Is the board operating this institution or are the professionals operating it?"

The bishop dropped his head to contemplate. Mrs. Purdy rose to the occasion. "Whether your insubordination is legal or not, young man, your behavior is shocking. You seem devoid of any righteous feeling of indignation at the immoral behavior of these girls. We on the board are people of quite different beliefs, but we can work together because we have a common, fundamental belief in morality. I doubt now that you believe in that morality, indeed, in any morality."

I looked at Bishop Elder, who was mute and defeated

because peace was not possible. I unleashed all the anger I had saved. "Mrs. Purdy, what you ladies on this board have in common is a desire to cleanse your own dirty consciences by punishing children who do what you do, or what you dream of doing."

It satisfied me to see them, mouths open but speechless. I turned to Bishop Elder, "Sir, please accept my resignation from this position. I have delayed much longer than I should have because I felt needed by the girls. But professional work is now impossible. In fact, the present situation would be ludicrous, were not the stakes in human life so high. You, as a committee of amateurs, have no business administering anything. Your task is to put the administration in the hands of competent administrators and leave it there.

"It is not enough that you meddle in administration. You also meddle in professional work. We shall all be fortunate if the harm you have done to the girls in this institution can be repaired. You have destroyed my usefulness. Go home, before you destroy the usefulness of other honest and competent people on this staff. You should name one professional person you can trust to administer, and go home. Go home before you cause a disaster."

"We accept your resignation with pleasure," Lola said.

"Please excuse me," I said. "I shall finish the job of emptying my desk, which you so kindly began." I turned to the bishop. "I don't believe, Bishop Elder, there is any reason to prolong everyone's agony. I only need to reassure myself of the welfare of a few girls and say a civilized good-by to them. I shall leave today."

The bishop lifted a shaking hand to his head and said, "Yes, of course, Doctor."

I composed myself in my office. I began to feel depressed and wanted to go home to Bonnie and the children. I tried to shake off the depression and then went downstairs to isolation.

When I stepped into the lower hall it was quiet. I stood a moment and felt myself lost again in time. Then I walked quietly down the hall a few steps and was about to knock on Jeannine's door.

"Is that you, Doc?" Rene called through the crack at the base of her door. "Can you talk to me now?"

"Yes, it's me, Rene. Are you all right?"

"Sure, I'm O.K., but I'm lonesome. Why did they move Jeannine?"

"They moved her?"

"Yeah, they moved her way down the hall."

"I don't know why, Rene. Look, I'll see you later."

I started down the hall slowly, fighting my own thoughts. It was beyond believing that anyone could cage this child, this tiny sad girl.

I opened the door to the big room. The light was dim, but the cage became visible, and hanging by the neck from its top was the fragile figure of Jeannine, hopelessly limp, the agony of violent death still on her face.